THUNDER ON THE TUNDRA

Inuit Qaujimajatuqangit of the Bathurst Caribou

Natasha Thorpe

Naikak Hakongak

Sandra Eyegetok

Kitikmeot Elders

Ikaluktuuttiak, Nunavut

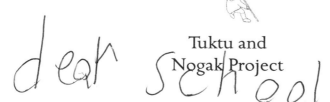

Tuktu and
Nogak Project

Second printing with updated material March 2002.

Maps generated by Kitikmeot GeoSciences Ltd.

NATIONAL LIBRARY OF CANADA CATALOGUING IN PUBLICATION DATA

Thorpe, Natasha
  Thunder on the tundra: Inuit qaujimajatuqangit of the Bathurst caribou

  Includes bibliographical references.
  ISBN 0-9689636-0-9

  1. Caribou—Nunavut—Bathurst Inlet Region. 2. Caribou—Nunavut—Kitikmeot Region. 3. Caribou hunting—Nunavut—Kitikmeot Region. 4. Inuit—Hunting—Nunavut—Kitikmeot Region. 5. Inuit—Ethnozoology—Nunavut—Kitikmeot Region. 6. Caribou—Parturition—Nunavut—Kitikmeot Region.

  I. Eyegetok, Sandra II. Hakongak, Naikak III. Tuktu and Nogak Project. IV. Title.

E99. E7T467 2001   599.65'8'0899712071955   C2001-902959-4

Typesetting and design: Lynn O'Rourke
Copy editor: Naomi Pauls
Illustrations: Kitikmeot elders and youth. See page 204.
Front cover photograph and interior colour photographs: Paul Nicklen
Back cover photographs: Natasha Thorpe, Sandra Eyegetok, Naikak Hakongak
Photographs of elders: Natasha Thorpe, Sandra Eyegetok, David Pelly, and Bob Bromley
Other duotone photographs: Natasha Thorpe, Sandra Eyegetok, David Pelly, and Bob Bromley

See also illustration credits on page 204.

Printed and bound in Vancouver by Generation Printing.

For more information or book orders please see www.polarnet.ca/tuktu or tnp1@hotmail.com

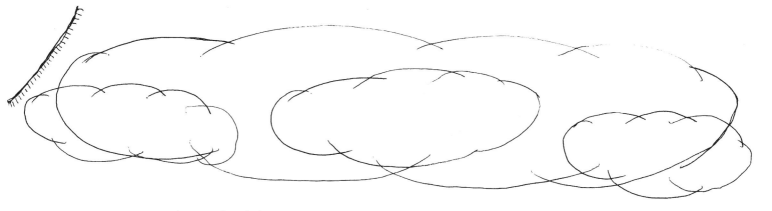

A more detailed version of this chronicle was submitted to the West Kitikmeot/Slave Study Society and can be viewed at *www.wkss.nt.ca.*

Contributors to the Tuktu and Nogak Project include:

PRINCIPAL TRANSLATOR AND TRANSCRIBER: Mary Kaosoni

CONTRIBUTOR: Margo Kadlun-Jones

TRANSLATORS AND TRANSCRIBERS: Doris Angohaitok, Martha Angulalik, Sandra Eyegetok, Margo Kadlun-Jones, Eileen Kakolak, Mary Kaosoni, Eva Komak, John Komak, and James Panioyak

PRINCIPAL RESEARCHER: Natasha Thorpe

SENIOR RESEARCHERS: Sandra Eyegetok, Naikak Hakongak, and Margo Kadlun-Jones

INTERVIEWERS: Sandra Eyegetok, Naikak Hakongak, Nancy Haniliak, Eileen Kakolak, Myste Kamingoak, Eva Komak, Meyok Omilgoitok, Karen Ongahak, and Natasha Thorpe

REVIEWERS: Bobby Algona, Jack Alonak, Gerry Atatahak, Gord Comer, Douglas Fugger, Chris Hanks, Margo Kadlun-Jones, Gary Kofinas, Jimmy Maniyogina, Cristina Soto, and Doug Stern

PHOTOGRAPHERS: Bob Bromley, Sandra Eyegetok, Paul Nicklen, David Pelly, and Natasha Thorpe

To the Kitikmeot elders and hunters who generously shared their valuable insights into Inuit traditions and their intimate relationship with caribou. Through the Tuktu and Nogak Project, you have provided a window into the Inuit ways of yesterday for all peoples today and tomorrow.

Contents

PAUL NICKLEN

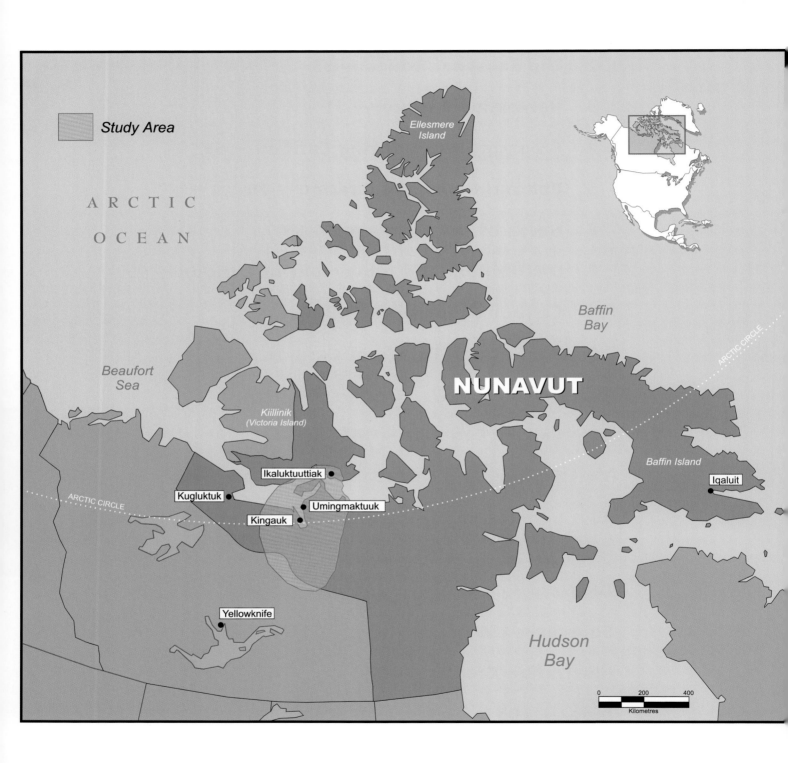

Study Area

ARCTIC OCEAN

Ellesmere Island

Beaufort Sea

Baffin Bay

NUNAVUT

ARCTIC CIRCLE

Kiillinik (Victoria Island)

Baffin Island

Ikaluktuuttiak

Iqaluit

Kugluktuk

Umingmaktuuk

Kingauk

ARCTIC CIRCLE

Yellowknife

Hudson Bay

0   200   400
Kilometres

Maps

Tables

Appendices

Acknowledgements

It is difficult to imagine that what started as a conversation over tea led to a major study documenting Qitirmiut knowledge of caribou in the Kitikmeot region. Five years later, we present *Thunder on the Tundra: Inuit Qaujimajatuqangit of the Bathurst Caribou*. Through our effort, we hope that all Qitirmiut will feel pride in celebrating and passing on their wisdom. This unique knowledge, Inuit Qaujimajatuqangit, will guide northerners concerned with caribou in the Kitikmeot region.

For us, the Tuktu and Nogak Project has been an exceptional and rewarding challenge from start to finish. We hope that this chronicle is just the dawn of many more efforts to share Inuit Qaujimajatuqangit.

We have tried to retain the voice of our co-authors, Kitikmeot elders. Thus, the information throughout this chronicle comes from elders and hunters who were interviewed for the Tuktu and Nogak Project, unless otherwise stated.

Kitikmeot elders and other community members have taught us a lifetime of stories in our moments sharing *mukpauyaq* and *mipku* (fry bread and dry meat). *Quana* for your laughter, brilliance, patience, forgiveness, graciousness, and compassion. You have shown us a glimpse of the ocean through a crack in the sea ice.

On behalf of the Tuktu and Nogak Board, we wish to thank everybody who shared their knowledge and experiences with the Tuktu and Nogak Project. We are grateful to the elders and other community members who gave us the faith and support we needed to make the project a success. We hope we have made you proud.

The Tuktu and Nogak Project relied upon a unique collaboration between elders, hunters, youth, researchers, and academics from the initial stages of community consultation to the production of this final report. Such co-operation would not have been possible without the enormous camaraderie, trust, and dedication demonstrated by many people.

Interviews with hunters and elders were led by Sandra Eyegetok, Naikak Hakongak, Nancy Haniliak, Eileen Kakolak, Myste Kamingoak, Eva Komak, Meyok Omilgoitok, Karen Ongahak, and Natasha Thorpe. Transcription and translation services were provided by Doris Angohaitok, Martha Angulalik, Sandra Eyegetok, Margo Kadlun-Jones, Eileen Kakolak, Mary Kaosoni, Eva Komak, John Komak, and James Panioyak. On the recommendation of many elders, local students were encouraged to learn from their elders while working for the Tuktu and Nogak Project. These students included Christine Agligoetok, Jason Akoluk, Ovik Akoluk, Tommy Akoluk, Arnold Angivrana, Yvonne Angohaitok, Shauna Angulalik, Thomas Apsimik, Bobby Ayalik, Tasha Daniels, Allison Evetaligak, Karen Kamoayok, Zane Kaniak, Doris Keyok, George Keyok, Joseph Keyok, Corey Klengenberg, Vanna Klengenberg, Janice Komak, Neal Mala, Pitik Niptanatiak, Donna Tikhak, and Joseph Tikhak Jr.

Quotes within this chronicle are from interviews with the following elders and hunters from four communities and one outpost camp in the Kitikmeot region:

HANIGAKHIK (BROWN SOUND)
>Alice Kingnektak, Doris Kingnektak

IKALUKTUUTTIAK (CAMBRIDGE BAY)
>Frank Analok, Bessie Angulalik, Mabel Angulalik,
>Naikak Hakongak, Annie Kaosoni, Mackie Kaosoni,
>David Kaniak, George Kavanna, Moses Koihok,
>Annie Komak, Archie Komak, Jimmy Maniyogina,
>Bessie Omilgoitok, Paul Omilgoitok

KINGAUK (BATHURST INLET)
>Martha Akoluk, Jessie Hagialok,
>George Kapolak Haniliak, Allen Kapolak, Anonymous C

KUGLUKTUK (COPPERMINE)
>Bobby Algona, May Algona, Jack Alonak, Nellie Hikok,
>Buster Kailik, Connie Nalvana

UMINGMAKTUUK (BAY CHIMO)
>John Akana, Nancy Haniliak, Lena Kamoayok, Mary Kaniak,
>Charlie Keyok, Mona Keyok, George Kuptana, Noah Kuptana,
>Ella Panegyuk, George Panegyuk

The final report was a collaborative writing effort by Natasha Thorpe, Naikak Hakongak, Sandra Eyegetok and Kitikmeot elders and hunters, with contributions from Margo Kadlun-Jones. The first draft was reviewed by members of the Tuktu and Nogak Project Writing Committee, namely Bobby Algona, Jack Alonak, and Jimmy Maniyogina. Gerry Atatahak, Chris Hanks, and Gary Kofinas also generously contributed their comments. The second draft was edited by Gord Comer, Douglas Fugger, Cristina Soto, and Doug Stern. Inuinnaqtun-speaking members of the committee Paul Omilgoitok of Ikaluktuuttiak and Mary Kaniak of Umingmaktuuk will review a translated copy of this text.

Illustrations for this book were created during several elder-youth drawing workshops held in communities for this purpose. Contributing artists were AJ Aknavigak, May Algona, Alice Anablak, Frank Analok, Catherine Anayoak, Alice Ayalik, Sandra Eyegetok, Bessie Hayohok, Nellie Hikok, McCotter Ihumatak, Christopher Ilgok, Buster Kailik, Becky Kakolak, Koaha Kakolak, Nathan Kakolak, Logan Kaniak, Loretta Kaniak, Mary Kaniak, Jack Kaodluak, Bella Kapolak, Chad Keadjuk, Adam Kikpak, Mary Kilaodluk, Matthew Kokak, Annie Komak, Connie Nalvana, Pitik Niptanatiak, Teddy Novoligak, Bessie Omilgoitok, Jim Oniak, Aivgak Pedersen, Elva Pigalak, and Julian Tologanak.

Arctic photographers Paul Nicklen and David Pelly charitably contributed several photos found throughout this chronicle. Natasha Thorpe, Sandra Eyegetok, and Bob Bromley supplied additional photos.

The Tuktu and Nogak Project was a tremendous example of individuals and agencies working together for a common goal, and would not have been possible without the dedication of several key people. We would like to give enormous thanks to Stanley Anablak, Gerry Atatahak, Patty Bligh, Sandy Buchan, Sarath Chandrasekre, Luke Coady, Gord Comer, Grant Corey, Kim Crockatt, James Eetoolook, Charlie Evalik, Chris Hanks, Betty Harnum, Jack Kaniak, Gary Kofinas, David Livingstone, Allen Maghagak, Hal Mills, Jack Meyok Omilgoitok, Lynn O'Rourke, Damian Panayi, Naomi Pauls, David Pelly, Evelyn Pinkerton, Shane Sather, Rose Spicker, Doug Stern, Alex Thomson, Leslie Tse, Mary Whelen-Grey, and Mindy Willett. We apologize if we have forgotten anybody, but there is such a long list of people who have helped us out! We appreciate each and every one of your contributions.

Many others participated in public meetings and provided important guidance. Thank you to Edith Aklok, Betty Ahegona, Mary Akana, Alice and George Anablak, Annie and Steve Anavilok, Sam Angnahiak, Doris and Gary Angohaitok, Sarah Atigiyoak, Mona Aviak, Junna Ehaloak, Shirley Elias, Bessie Emingak, Lena Evalik, Mona Evetaligak, Ruby and Jimmy Haniliak, Connie Hatogina, Bessie Hayokhok, Jack Hikhaitok, Kate Inuktalik, Jack Itikhaitok, Connie Kapolak, Martina and Peter Kapolak, Susie and Sam Kapolak, Mona Kigiuna, Lena and Sam Kikpak, Gwen and Allen Kitigon, Emma and Clarence Klengenberg, June Klengenberg, Laura Kohoktak, Luke Kudlak, Alice Kuptana, Jimmy Nakoyak, Jessie Neglak, Tasha Neglak, Luke Noviligak, Sarah Novoligak, Mamie Oniak, Jack Ovilok, George Panegyuk, William Pigalak, Annie and Walter Pokiak, Mona Tigitkok, Mona Tiktalik, Gwen and Joseph Tikhak, Jeannie Tologanak, and Amos Wamikun.

We are grateful to the following agencies for recognizing the value of Inuit Qaujimajatuqangit and respecting the process of community-driven research.

MAJOR
CONTRIBUTORS

Association of Canadian Universities for Northern Studies

BHP Minerals Incorporated

Department of Sustainable Development, Government of Nunavut

Indian and Northern Affairs Canada, Government of Canada

Kitikmeot Inuit Association

Northern Scientific Training Program

Nunavut Tunngavik Incorporated

Nunavut Wildlife Management Board

Social Science and Humanities Research Council

West Kitikmeot / Slave Study Society

SIGNIFICANT
CONTRIBUTORS

Arctic Institute of North America

Education, Culture and Employment, Government of the NWT

Hamlet of Ikaluktuuttiak

Kitikmeot Economic Development Corporation

Nunavut Planning Commission

ADDITIONAL
SUPPORT AND
CONTRIBUTIONS-
IN-KIND

Calm Air

Co-Op Stores

Ekaluktutiak Hunters and Trappers Organization

First Air

Government of Nunavut

Kingaok Hunters and Trappers Organization

Kitikmeot GeoSciences Limited

Kitikmeot Heritage Society

Kugluktuk Angoniatit Association

Northern Store

Nunavut Arctic College

Nunavut Impact Review Board

Omingmaktok Hunters and Trappers Organization

Polarnet

Simon Fraser University

Finally, our family and friends have given us their unconditional love and support over the years. You were brave in accepting our moods and absences! For Uaakkallaaluga, you are the crimson sunrise that dances fire on the horizon and lures me home from the long, cold, and dark Arctic night. For Donna, Ovilok, and Nuka, a heartfelt thanks for enduring my time away from home. For Henriguluq, quana for your patience, understanding, and support. Thanks also to Bella Rose and Jorgen. Thank you to Howie, our daughters Lauren and Caley, and the many people who took part in the interviews—*quanaqpiaquhi*.

—Natasha Thorpe, Sandra Eyegetok,
Naikak Hakongak, and Margo Kadlun-Jones
Ikaluktuuttiak, July 2000

Ayaa-ya-ya

Ayaa-ya-ya-ya-yaa

Yaa

Yaa

Yaa-a!

These sounds echo into the midnight sun as Inuit elders and youth gather to watch Jack Alonak drum dance. He hops from one foot to the other with a limber grace that betrays his years. Other elders sing along with the same tireless energy while youth clap and giggle. Young twins, Becky and Nathan, stand motionless, mouths agape, while grasping onto the tent lines for balance. Soon Jack pauses to explain the olden time song he sings and everybody listens—even the lone bull caribou that watches from the bank across the river as if invited. And he is.

—Researchers' Notes,
Hiukkittaak Elder-Youth Camp,
August 1998

Introduction

This book is by and for the Kitikmeot elders and hunters involved in the Tuktu and Nogak Project (TNP), which translates as the Caribou and Calves Project. The TNP was a community-driven effort to communicate and document local Qitirmiut (Inuit) knowledge of mainland caribou in the Kitikmeot region of Nunavut (see Appendix A). Interviews were held in English and Inuinnaqtun between 1996 and 2000 with thirty-seven elders and hunters from Ikaluktuuttiak (Cambridge Bay), Kingauk (Bathurst Inlet), Kugluktuk (Coppermine), Umingmaktuuk (Bay Chimo), and the outpost camp of Hanigakhik (Brown Sound).

Through interviews, community members shared their insights, observations, experiences, wisdom, and stories about caribou (see APPENDIX B for a list of the interview questions). Each interview was transcribed, translated, and read aloud back to the elder or hunter for verification. People marked on 1:250,000 maps covered in clear plastic their traditional hunting, fishing, camping, and travelling grounds important to their stories. This knowledge was entered into a database of maps and text that form the backbone of this book. We have tried to retain the voice of the elders and hunters by editing their quotes as little as possible.

The Need for a Study

Numerous circumstances led to the need for a project to document and share Inuit ecological knowledge of caribou and calving areas in the Kitikmeot region. First, individuals who were conducting an extensive traditional knowledge study (the Naonayaotit Traditional Knowledge Study, NTKS) realized that their study was too broad to provide detailed information on caribou and calving areas in the Bathurst Inlet region. At the same time, many interviewees mentioned that caribou were of particular importance and interest. In order to address these concerns, Gerry Atatahak, principal researcher for the study, suggested that another research project be undertaken to focus on caribou and calving areas.

In the North, elders are passing away while youth, more fluent in English than Inuinnaqtun, struggle to live on the land, speak their language, and learn from their elders. Inuit knowledge held by elders represents intergenerational wisdom that spans many spatial and temporal boundaries. Loss of this understanding would be detrimental to Inuit culture in general, and to the sustainable management of northern lands, resources, and wildlife in particular.

Wildlife resources are critical to northerners, who depend upon healthy populations of animals for hunting, ceremony, and tradition. For the Qitirmiut, caribou are of particular relevance, since the herd migrates through and calves in traditional Qitirmiut lands.

Mineral exploration and the potential for mine development provide an additional reason for seeking a comprehensive understanding of Inuit knowledge of caribou in the region. Ultimately, local and historical information about caribou documented through this project will assist northern communities, agencies, and interest groups in making decisions related to mineral development, lands, resources, and wildlife.

Throughout the many stages of the TNP, guiding goals were to ensure a high level of community consultation, to remain flexible to local input, and to foster opportunities for youth involvement. After several months of community consultation, both formal and informal, community members nominated representatives to sit on an advisory board called the Tuktu and Nogak Board (TNB). The TNB gave the study a name, defined its goals and structure, and suggested people who could be trained as staff. The TNB met regularly and directed the TNP through all stages. Throughout the project, community members were consulted frequently and the TNP was adapted upon their recommendations. Details of the research process can be found in a longer version of this book available through *www.wkss.nt.ca*, or by request from *tnp1@hotmail.com*

Community members suggested that trips on the land would be the best place to record stories, as this is where people hunt and observe caribou. As a result, an elder-youth camp was held on the Hiukkittaak River during the summer of 1998 with the assistance of the Kitikmeot Inuit Association. The camp provided opportunities for researchers to record traditional stories and observations of caribou. It also brought together elders and youth from different communities to strengthen Inuit culture. The camp was key to involving youth in the TNP.

THE HIUKKITTAAK ELDER-YOUTH CAMP, HIUKKITTAAK RIVER, 1998.

The Hiukkittaak Elder-Youth Camp provided an exceedingly good source of information for the TNP. On the land, it was both easy and enjoyable for elders to share their knowledge of and experience with caribou and calving areas, to demonstrate caribou and people interactions (for example hunting, butchering, and skinning), and to spend quality time with the younger generation. Elders led the camp by sharing what they felt was most important for the youth to learn through demonstration, rather than by responding to what other people determined was valuable, as can be the case with a questionnaire. Details of the camp are reported in both Inuinnaqtun and English in other sources (Thorpe 1998; Thorpe and Eyegetok 1998, 2000a, 2000b).

Inuit Qaujimajatuqangit

Although Western science-based research provides much information about caribou, less attention has been given to how these animals are observed, experienced, and explained by the Inuit. This local or traditional knowledge, known as Inuit Qaujimajatuqangit (IQ), has been poorly recorded historically. The TNP was an effort to document this knowledge, thus contributing to a new understanding of caribou.

Inuit Qaujimajatuqangit is "what has always been known"—Inuit knowledge, insight, and wisdom that is gained through experience, shared through stories, and passed from one generation to the next. More than just knowledge, as commonly defined, IQ includes a finely tuned awareness of the ever-changing relationship between Inuit and *nuna* (the land), *hila*, (the weather), wildlife, and the spiritual world.

Beyond "what has always been known," IQ can also be translated as "what [Inuit] must or have to know." It is essential knowledge that incorporates "beliefs." IQ is infused with spirituality, and grounded in respect and animism as well as more recent traditions such as those from the Anglican and Roman Catholic Church. Throughout the TNP, there were many cases when elders and hunters explained strange happenings on the nuna or with hila in a spiritual context. For example, Mary Kaniak (1998) told of a bull who came so close to the community of Kingauk that it must have been a relative coming to visit and should not be harvested. In IQ, the overlap of observations and beliefs is welcomed.

The fact that IQ spans generations distinguishes it from other ways of knowing and makes it valuable as a contribution to our understanding of caribou. Experiential knowledge, insights, and skills that were specific to the Qitirmiut way of life have passed the test of time and remain in use today.

IQ is also based on repeated local observations. These observations may or may not have relevance on a regional or global scale, but they do contribute significantly at the local level. Qitirmiut make their observations on a local scale and do not apply these to unfamiliar areas. This is, in part, because people are not comfortable speaking about that which they have not seen, and they do not want to mislead others or pass along second- or third-hand information.

THE FLUID NATURE OF IQ

As we listened to stories, we noticed how IQ was continuously expanding and changing depending on the person. IQ passed from one generation to the next is filtered through the listener and understood within the listener's experience or ability. Thus, IQ of the past is contributed to that of the present. In the 1990s, IQ

expanded to include everything from political change with the creation of Nunavut to climate change, with new observations of variations in weather, water, land, and wildlife.

Through the TNP and within this book, we have taken IQ from the oral to the written domain. In this process it may be that the complexities, interconnectedness, and additional wealth of information that characterize IQ are partially lost. This is because of difficulties inherent in the interview process, because of translation, and because some essence is necessarily lost when IQ is written down rather than explained, demonstrated, or acquired through experience.

In some ways, recording IQ on paper "freezes" IQ, and the "magic" conveyed through oral versus written traditions vanishes. Indeed, the written form should never be a replacement for the oral teaching and actual learning or acquiring of IQ. A young boy will learn more from watching and listening to his grandfather hunt a caribou and then experiencing the hunt himself than from reading a book about hunting. However, given that IQ is not fixed in one era but is continuously updated and enhanced by current observations, much IQ can be lost when it is not recorded. In the current world, documentation is the next best way to ensure that IQ is accessible to future generations.

Inuktitut is part of the Eskimo–Aleut language family and is spoken, in some form, from Siberia to Greenland. Inuinnaqtun is a dialect of the Inuktitut language primarily spoken in the Kitikmeot region. This book documents IQ shared by a specific group of Inuit (peoples of Inuit descent living in the Canadian Arctic) from the Kitikmeot region. The people of this region are referred to as Qitirmiut.

There are two methods of writing Inuinnaqtun: a newer and sanctioned system (standard Roman orthography) supported by the Government of Nunavut, and an older system that was originally taught in Anglican and Roman Catholic mission schools. This older system, used mostly by elders today, is not consistent so there can be many different spellings for the same word. One reason for the new system is to standardize spellings so that the written word better represents the actual sounds of Inuinnaqtun.

While elders and middle-aged people prefer the old Inuinnaqtun, the newer orthography is used in Nunavut schools, colleges, and governments. Using the new writing system, a non-Inuinnaqtun speaker, with a little study and practice, could learn how to pronounce an Inuinnaqtun word by sounding out the letters.

ALLEN KAPOLAK AND FRIENDS, ANIAGHIUGVIK, 1998.

INUINNAQTUN IN THIS CHRONICLE

If the written word actually represents the Inuinnaqtun sounds, it may be easier for people to retain their language and speak across dialects, long after the fluent Inuinnaqtun speakers have passed away. Many people resist changing to the new Inuinnaqtun writing system, despite the fact that the language is being lost.

For these reasons, and to support the official Government of Nunavut directive, we use the new Inuinnaqtun wherever possible. However, choosing spellings for place names posed a particular challenge. Out of respect for the elders and to ease collaboration with other heritage projects (for example, Kitikmeot Heritage Society projects and the NTKS), we have used the old rather than new spellings for place names. APPENDIX A lists other spellings and English names for places. MAPS 1A and 1B both illustrate traditional place names in the Kitikmeot region, many of which continue to be significant camping, hunting, or heritage areas. These place names appear on two maps simply because they would not all fit on one. Elders and hunters referred to these places, often by pointing to maps, frequently throughout the interviews. That there are numerous places mentioned in the quotes in this book reflects how critical the land continues to be for most Qitirmiut.

Since most interviews were conducted in Inuinnaqtun, then translated into English, the quotes throughout this chronicle may not perfectly represent the ideas of the interviewee. This is because many Inuinnaqtun words do not translate into English without some shift in their meaning. For example, the word "*hila*" is usually translated as "weather" or "the outdoors," while it actually embodies much more than this: hila includes the relationships between Inuit, climate, weather, plants, wildlife, spirits, and the land. Similarly, the word "*nuna*" is typically translated as "land," when most people say that nuna includes not only the land, but also the relationships between the land and other biological, spiritual, and physical elements of the tundra.

GERRY ATATAHAK,
KUGLUKTUK, 1999.

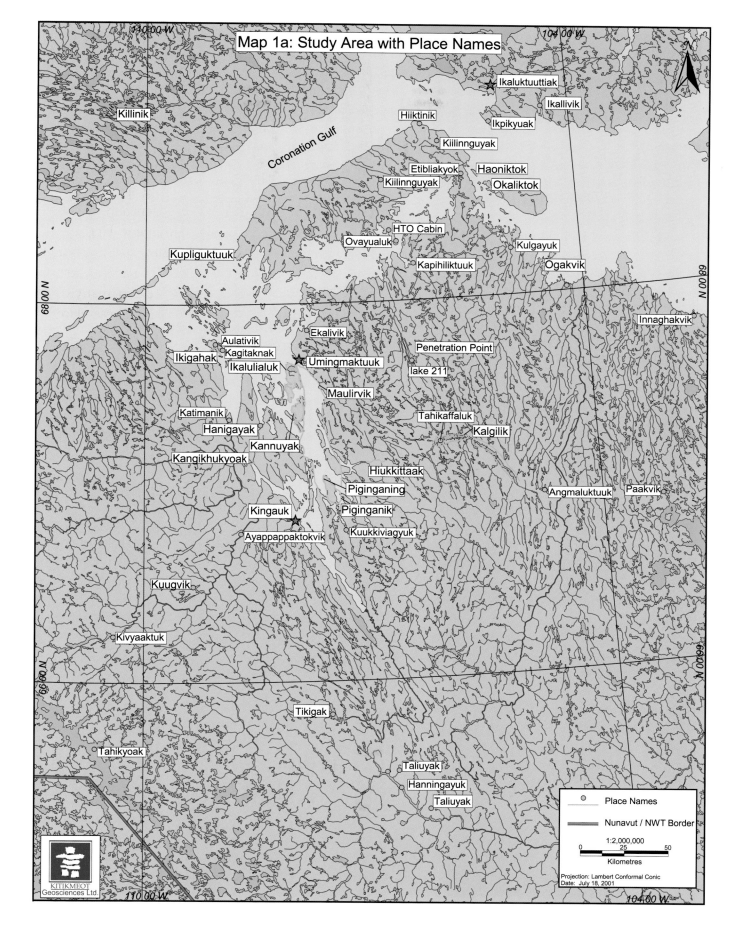

Map 1a: Study Area with Place Names

Coronation Gulf

Killinik
Ikaluktuuttiak
Ikallivik
Ikpikyuak
Hiiktinik
Kiilinnguyak
Etibliakyok
Haoniktok
Kiilinnguyak
Okaliktok
HTO Cabin
Ovayualuk
Kulgayuk
Kupliguktuuk
Kapihiliktuuk
Ogakvik
Innaghakvik
Ekalivik
Aulativik
Penetration Point
Kagitaknak
Ikigahak
Umingmaktuuk
lake 211
Ikalulialuk
Maulirvik
Katimanik
Tahikaffaluk
Hanigayak
Kalgilik
Kannuyak
Kangikhukyoak
Hiukkittaak
Piginganing
Paakvik
Kingauk
Piginganik
Angmaluktuuk
Ayappappaktokvik
Kuukkiviagyuk
Kuugvik
Kivyaaktuk
Tikigak
Tahikyoak
Taliuyak
Hanningayuk
Taliuyak

Place Names
Nunavut / NWT Border
1:2,000,000
0   25   50
Kilometres
Projection: Lambert Conformal Conic
Date: July 18, 2001

KITIKMEOT
Geosciences Ltd.

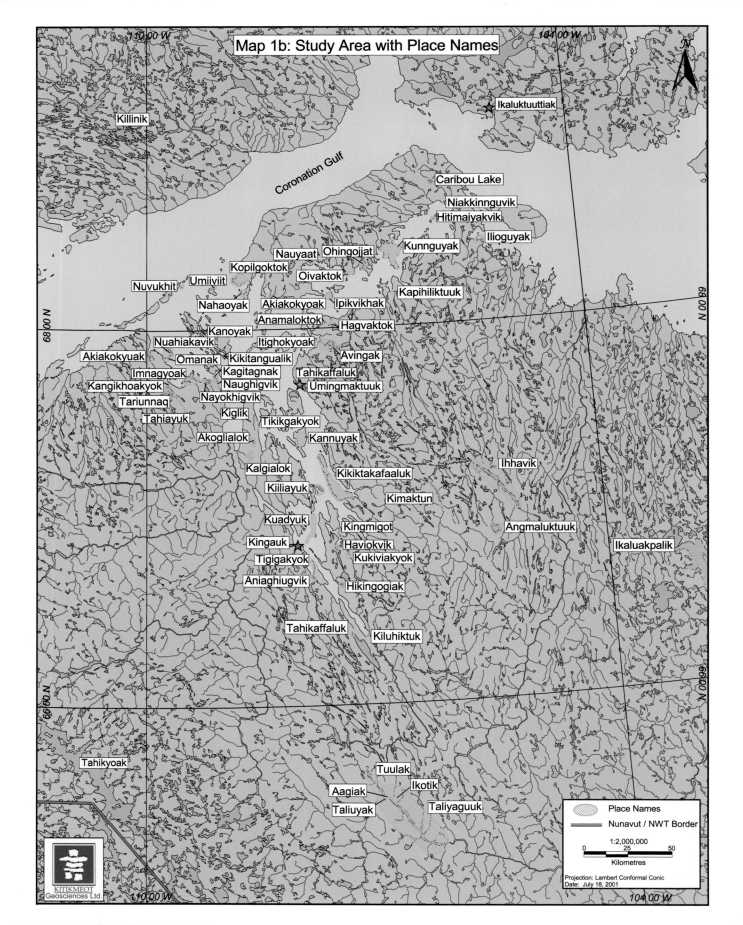

Map 1b: Study Area with Place Names

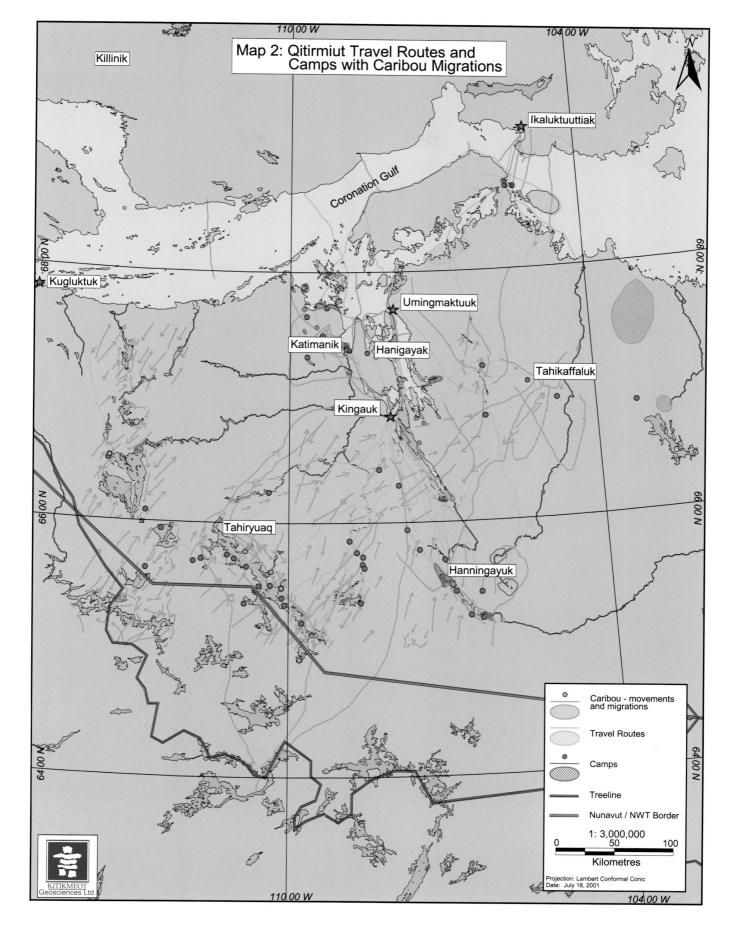

Map 2: Qitirmiut Travel Routes and Camps with Caribou Migrations

PAUL NICKLEN

The land of the Kitikmeot region is typical tundra, marked in some places by gently undulating hills and meadows covered in grasses, sedges, and low-lying shrubs. Bathurst Inlet is particularly unique in the number of great rock outcrops that tower over the landscape. The Kitikmeot is the most westerly region of the three regions in Nunavut established by the Nunavut Land Claims Agreement. It covers an area of nearly a quarter of a million square kilometres of tundra, lakes, and ocean, most of it north of the Arctic Circle. All the maps in this book were generated from the TNP textual and spatial database, which was based on elders' and hunters' markings.

From the outset, Kitikmeot elders and hunters have provided input and direction to the Tuktu and Nogak Project to ensure that Inuit Qaujimajatuqangit is recorded for present and future generations. Through the project, the value of IQ relating to caribou and calving grounds has emerged, especially in the areas of uniting elders and youth, preserving and promoting Inuit heritage, and documenting critical knowledge for informed decision-making about wildlife. The same determination, dedication, and insight of Qitirmiut that enabled their survival can be heard throughout *Thunder on the Tundra*. Listen.

ABOUT THE KITIKMEOT REGION

1 Inuit and Caribou

Although Qitirmiut lifestyles have changed today compared to long ago, caribou continue to be central to culture, identity, and diet. In traditional times, people moved with the caribou and set camps along their migration routes. This is particularly evident in MAP 2 (PAGE 9), which shows traditional Qitirmiut camps and travel routes along with caribou migrations.

Qitirmiut are no longer as nomadic and do not follow the caribou as they did in the past, yet they remain concerned about the health and condition of caribou, especially given modern-day social and environmental pressures.

Missionaries and traders settled in the Kitikmeot region between 1910 and 1920. Small settlements sprang up at Katimanik (Arctic Sound), Kingauk, Kuugyuak (Perry River), Warrender Bay, Western River, and Wilmot Island. In those days, Qitirmiut families spent most summers and winters inland as far south as the Back River and Contwoyto Lake. People usually visited the trading posts at Christmas and Easter. In the 1940s, after the trading posts started to sell boats and small motors, people moved to the coast for the summer.

> We were at Katimanik for a while and had fun. We would walk and collect eggs around here.... We were there for many summers because there are fish and caribou there. We would go here in the spring and in August we would move elsewhere to trap.... We were alone with [the] Uqaittuqs, Amiraiqniqs, Kullaqs, Utuqiaqs, and Quahas at the [caribou] crossings.
>
> *Nellie Hikok, 1999*

> People would spend the winter inland until the spring.... They would spend the winter inland in caribou skin tents.... There would be many tents side by side in the spring when the people gathered to pick up supplies from the posts preparing to go inland. People would go to the ocean and hunt seal for boots. They hunted seals and bearded seals for boots that they would use to walk inland in the summer up past Kingauk towards Hanningayuk (Beechey Lake). They would reach Hanningayuk walking with all the mosquitoes around. Dogs would be packing supplies.
>
> *George Kuptana, 1998*

Once the posts were established, people exchanged their furs for goods such as flour, guns, stoves, sugar, tea, tobacco, and traps. Qitirmiut built small houses using wood from the crates shipped to the posts or washed up on shore.

We would use the fox pelts to buy what we needed, as well as wolves, wolverines, red foxes, cross foxes. We did not see any cash then. When people needed stuff a long time ago, they would use matchsticks as markers for the foxes they used to trade with. After the foxes were prepared, the people would be given matchsticks to use when they needed stuff. After the clerk documented the number of foxes, he would give the trapper a number of sticks.... When I was younger I used to trade like that. When I was younger, I did not have a lot of traps so I got a few foxes.... I bought myself a record player that winds. I enjoyed that. I stored it on the sled; only when we stopped to camp I would use it. There were two things that I most enjoyed—that and my watch.

Frank Analok, 1999

During the 1940s and 1950s, some families began travelling less and spending more time in the Kingauk area. Qitirmiut gathered at Hanigakhik (Brown Sound), Kanikhuakyuk (Daniel Moore Bay), Katimanik, Nauyaat (Parry Bay), Kingauk, and Umingmaktuuk. In the 1960s, the federal government erected prefabricated houses in Umingmaktuuk, and people began staying in these new houses in the winter while going out to their favourite hunting and fishing areas during the rest of the year, especially in the summer.

In the mid-1960s, the trading post in Kingauk was moved to Umingmaktuuk and soon was modernized to become a store. In the 1970s, a school was established in Umingmaktuuk and a tourist lodge was built in Kingauk. Today, these two communities are dwindling quickly as people move towards the larger centres of Kugluktuk and Ikaluktuuttiak (Cambridge Bay), which are serviced by medical facilities and schools. Between 1996 and 2001, the population of Umingmaktuuk was reduced by three-quarters. Kingauk and Umingmaktuuk are commonly labelled as two of the most "traditional" communities because people subsist largely on country foods, speak Inuinnaqtun frequently, live without running water, and use generators for electricity (since the 1980s).

There has always been a kindred relationship of gratitude and respect felt by Qitirmiut for caribou. With the caribou migrations, people are grateful for the long-awaited meat, skins, and other bounty that is soon eaten or transformed into tents and clothing. Further, people can become animals in the afterlife, which is another reason to respect caribou.

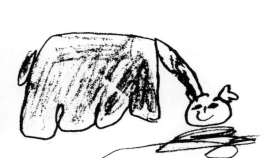

> [Inuit] say that relatives, a close brother or close father or sister or whatever, that recently passed away.... If they ever die, one day they are going to come back to this place. And I heard of a bear coming to camp and being very shy and everybody had a rifle on him, but he was trying to tell the people that he was not harmful or not going to eat anybody. Something clicked in one of the person's minds, who said, "Oh yeah, maybe it is my grandfather coming to visit."…. Even birds would come right into the house and sit up, just watch, watch you move or the ceiling, stay there for a while and fly back out again, and some old folks say that their relatives that have recently passed away come for a visit.
>
> *Bobby Algona, 1999*

I heard of one person becoming a caribou. He dressed up as a caribou, trying to make himself look like a caribou to sneak up on caribou. So he got a caribou hide, put it on his face, and started to crawl to the caribou. Somehow the hide became the hide of that person, and that is how he became a caribou.... There was a certain thing he had to do if he wanted to come out of being a caribou, but he forgot what it was. And he became a caribou and he could not remember any more. The hardest thing that he ever did was try to dodge all those bulls and those teeth, how to stay right in the middle of the herd. He was always stumbling.... Then he remembered the old man telling him to keep his head high, just like a caribou. Caribou stays high when he is walking and running. So he started keeping his head high and not looking at the ground and started not stumbling any more. So he migrated with the herd for the winter, and springtime he migrated all the way back again. Then he remembered what to do in order to become a person again. The way he remembered, he said, was he saw that person hunting that told him, that old man that told him how to be caribou. "Oh yeah, that person told me how to do that." He did it and became a person again.

Bobby Algona, 1999

[Cows] are the same as humans. Like women do not have babies after they have reached a certain age, that is how it is with caribou as well.

Archie Komak, 1998

When a calf is born before reaching the calving grounds, they [cows] would take care of their young like people do. Like a person would.

Mackie Kaosoni, 1999

CARIBOU CAN BECOME PEOPLE, AND THERE ARE MANY COMPARISONS MADE BETWEEN CARIBOU AND PEOPLE.

Annie Komak,
Bessie Omilgoitok,
Mary Kaniak,
and John Akana,
Hiukkittaak Elder-Youth
Camp, August 1998.

A Conversation between the Elders

RECORDED DURING THE
HIUKKITTAAK ELDER-YOUTH
CAMP, AUGUST 1998.

Mary Kaniak: [Caribou] become bulls after four years.... Maybe after six years, they start mating.... These boys [teenagers] are almost bulls.

Bessie Omilgoitok: You boys are going to turn into bulls pretty soon!

John Akana: These young people will find out when they have spouses. They will understand what we are talking about.

Caribou are not particularly bright animals, which is one of the reasons why they are hunted relatively easily. In comparison, the wolf, wolverine, and grizzly are respected for their cunning and strategic ways of fooling hunters.

> Caribou are not like people, and do not wait until [the ice] is solid.... [The caribou] were skinny. They had fallen into the water. Just after freeze-up they would go on the side [or shore of the lake]. They are not afraid. They do not think like people do.
>
> *George Kuptana, 1998*

Qitirmiut care about the health and survival of caribou. Two hunters in Kingauk told of a time when they helped a young calf that was struggling to swim across a long channel. They loaded the calf into the boat and drove it to shore. Another year, a group of barren and pregnant cows became stranded on an island in Bathurst Inlet and were helped by Qitirmiut.

> [In the early 1990s] caribou got stranded here on Rideout Island. They got stuck there so most of them died. They tried to cross back, but this whole island got wiped out because there was no grass left for them to eat.... Joseph Tikhak was there and he tried to help by bringing grass from the other side to the island. He would bring some to the island, but the caribou finished it right away.
>
> *Alice Kingnektak, 1998*

The acts of hunting, butchering, preparing, eating, and sharing the caribou harvest are important in uniting people, families, and generations. Qitirmiut give thanks to caribou for the way in which this animal provides for quality time spent together. Caribou is soul food, because of the way it brings happiness to the self and togetherness to the community.

Qitirmiut youth today do not harvest caribou as they had to in the past and therefore do not feel the pride and self-worth that is gained by participating in a caribou harvest. According to the elders, this is part of the reason why youth complain of being "bored" so often.

TABLE 1
Inuinnaqtun Names for Caribou

Since traditional times, Qitirmiut have honoured caribou for the ways in which this animal has contributed to Qitirmiut subsistence. Surviving on caribou meant that people had to recognize the many caribou throughout the stages in their lives. There are different names for various types of caribou.

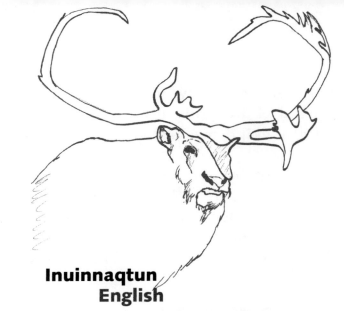

Inuinnaqtun
English

Iblau
Foetus

Nurraq,
Nurralaaq
Calf

Auyalingniq
Summer newborn calves

Nukatukkaaq
Yearling

Kulavak
Cow

Nurraittuq
Barren cow

Pangniq
Bull

Anguhalluq
Young bull

Upin'ngaaliq
Spring caribou

Kan'ngalaq
Spring caribou (when the old hair has fallen off the antlers)

Hagganguqtuq
Summer caribou (with some new hair on the antlers)

Ukiakharnitaq
Fall caribou

Pitiktaakkat
Winter caribou

Ahiarmiut
Mainland caribou

Kiillinik
Island caribou

Amiralik
Caribou (with velvet on the antlers)

Feelings of gratitude and respect for caribou may have been stronger in traditional times, when Qitirmiut depended on these animals for survival. Although some meat was wasted in traditional times, wastage was not as common as it is today. In the past, meat was scarce, whereas today there are other foods and wastage does not threaten survival. It may be that since caribou are easier to hunt today and have become "more tame," they appear to be more plentiful and therefore are considered less valuable. This may contribute to some people wasting caribou meat.

> Now they just leave the foetus with the rest of the
> remains when they bring a caribou home. I do not
> know, it is probably politically incorrect to do that!
> All that has to do with politics. It is just a difference
> of how people treat animals now they can go to the
> store and buy food.
>
> *Naikak Hakongak, 1998*

It is common nowadays for people to bring back caribou meat to their communities and leave parts of the hides, legs, heads, liver, and intestines at the kill site for scavengers to feast upon. In modern times, some people are discouraged by the amount of time and energy it takes to pack, dry, butcher, and process meat and hides.

> I break all traditions. Guts are always left. Parts of the
> meat that I cut off. Sometimes I forget to take out the
> kidneys or the liver. And I throw the lungs away and
> cut the throat right from the jaw right down to where it
> connects with the lungs. The bronchial tube. I always
> used to throw that away. What else do I throw away?
> Too much of it I guess. I never take the blood home to
> make blood soup. When my mom was alive, she used to
> always say, "Why do you not bring the blood home?"
> and I said, "I do not know. I did not bring a container
> for it." She used to always give us heck…. One time
> Tommy Kilaodluk got a caribou and brought it back

outside the house in Cambridge Bay. I guess my mom was complaining that she did not get some parts of the caribou that she really liked, so he went and got a caribou and took the blood out and took the parts that she wanted out and brought them in so she had a feast. She used to like the stomach contents.

Naikak Hakongak, 1998

WASTING
MEAT

Stemming from the days before modern conveniences and the availability of store-bought foods, many elders are accustomed to using all parts of the caribou. One elder expressed his worry about seeing many caribou, untouched except for their missing tongues, lying dead on the sea ice outside of Ikaluktuuttiak. Caribou tongues are considered a delicacy and one of the most favoured parts of the caribou. Other elders listening to this story shook their heads, talked about how this was "bad," and complained that some Qitirmiut today were not treating caribou with proper respect.

In the old days, when [Inuit] caught caribou, they used everything.... Their vegetables were the insides of the caribou stomach.... The tips of the antlers are just cartilage. I still eat those. There are lots of nutrients in that. The head, the cartilage in the head, the brains, the eyes, the ears.... Now they leave everything behind. There are different uses now than a long time ago. A long time ago, nothing was wasted. My mom still makes caribou feet when she can and I still eat caribou feet too. They are really fatty. Rubbery too. They are inside of the hooves you just pull it out.... I grew up in the era when we used to always ... try not to waste at all.

Naikak Hakongak, 1998

MABEL ANGULALIK,
IKALUKTUUTTIAK, 1998.

Inuit even cook the hooves. I just call it hooves, hoof stew, and eat the tendon out of that too just right in the hoof. They even cook the head and use the antlers for things like making some stuff to soften the caribou with or they could just use every part of the caribou. They eat the bone marrow and every part is used except for the guts.

Anonymous C, 1998

Sometimes there would be hard times when the caribou were scarce. The people from the land and the ocean would buy supplies during the spring. The people from inland would go to the ocean to catch seals to make boots from, water boots. People who lived inland would hunt seals for waterproof boots.

May Algona, 1999

Because [caribou are] the main source of food, people would never throw away caribou meat. There was not too much to hunt for food, so we never threw anything away except the stomach and the contents of the stomach. The intestines were used for food as well. The blood is used for broth…. The older people still cook and eat the head. The caribou heads are used for food as well. Sometimes the stomach would be eaten mixed with seal fat. Some elders still eat it today.

Frank Analok, 1998

When there was a large herd close by, people would hunt, sometimes without much sleep. They would get as many as they could to use for clothing. When the timing was right, during the migration, we would catch as many caribou as we could, which was used for clothing and food. That is what has been told.

Mabel Angulalik, 1998

In the past, there were strong traditions and rules, or *pitquhiit*, about not wasting meat. A breakdown in social customs and traditional lifestyle may contribute to younger people wasting meat.

> Once you start wasting caribou meat, you are going to
> have hard times in the future. So I try not to do those
> things, never do them anyway. I try to share my meat.
>
> *George Kavanna, 1999*

Today, in the spring, it is common for some meat to go to waste, especially recently, when sudden warm temperatures can spoil meat that has been stored frozen outside. Sometimes people do not have time to process the meat before it is covered in fly eggs and maggots. Spoiled meat that is not yet dangerous is often fed to dogs.

CARIBOU SHORTAGES: TIMES OF STARVATION

In traditional times, Qitirmiut lived on the land and moved according to the seasonal migration of the caribou because they counted on the caribou for food, shelter, clothes, tools, and, ultimately, much of what they needed to survive. People starved when the caribou migration failed to follow a traditional route, if wolverines or other animals raided meat caches, or if too much soft snow made travel—for both people and caribou—difficult. It is painful to talk about these times because of the memories of relatives and friends who starved.

> In the olden days, people used to throw away babies if
> they had no food to make them live. I was thrown away,
> too bad…. Qigarhana had to go along, she wanted to
> adopt me. She kept me alive.
>
> *George Kuptana, 1998*

GEORGE KUPTANA, UMINGMAKTUUK, 1997.

24

In the past when there was not much food inland during
the winter, people would come down to the ocean by dog
team, where there were seals and tomcod. People would
come down because they know there is game during
the winter.... Not too long ago, when there were a few
people left at Hanningayuk, when Ella Tunnuqahak's
husband and my parents were still alive, we spent our
last winter inland without food. We were having a hard
time back then. Even for far distances, there was no
wildlife. It must have been around May. There was
nothing to see close by. Nirlaaq reached our camp un-
noticed. We had been out of food for a long time. We
would catch a few fish, even a small amount, which
would not last, but we waited for people. We would take
the hair off caribou skins, cook them, and eat them.

John Akana, 1998

I remember we spent one fall near Hanningayuk
without food. I cannot remember much.... We were
without food and moved down from Hanningayuk.
It happened more than once.

Mary Kaniak, 1998

Traditional Uses of Caribou

CARIBOU PARTS WERE USED TO MAKE SURVIVAL EASIER IN THE PAST, BUT PEOPLE HAD TO BE ESPECIALLY CREATIVE AND CLEVER IN HOW THEY USED VARIOUS PARTS OF THE CARIBOU.

Caribou can be used for almost everything imaginable. Generally, skins are used for bedding, clothing, drums, kayaks, packs, rope, shelter, and sled runners. Antlers and bones are joined to pieces of sinew, rope, copper, or plastic and made into tools such as arrows, bows, harpoon heads, knives, fish hooks, or scrapers. While many of these uses have fallen out of favour due to modern equivalents, some grandparents and parents still try to teach their younger relatives about the older traditions.

It is much easier today to find clothing. In the old days, Qitirmiut women and girls made various types of clothing from caribou, depending on the occasion, in what season the caribou was harvested, or how the hide was prepared. Caribou hides can be made into parkas, inner and outer pants, boots, gloves, hats, diapers, menstrual pads, and more. Many people prefer the Kiillinik (Victoria Island) caribou for *kamngit* (boots) because they are thinner skinned, easier to scrape, and whitest in colour. Needles and thimbles were made from caribou bone.

Hunters select caribou for their furs during the late summer and early fall because this is when the caribou fur has a rich colour and does not shed as much. Further, wounds in the skin from warble fly larvae have healed. When the furs are used for clothing, the hunters cut them carefully and in particular ways. For example, legs from the caribou are used to make a pair of kamngit, for which eight legs are required.

> The people in the olden days would cache meat for the winter and use the skins for clothing, bedding. The furs would be properly skinned in the summer.
>
> *Annie Kaosoni, 1998*

> [Qitirmiut] make outer pants from cow skins because they are softer and easier to scrape. Bull skins are not used [as much] for clothing, but female and calf skins are used.
>
> *Lena Kamoayok, 1998*

In August, people would start hunting caribou for clothing when [the caribou] are heading south…. When the fur was not too thick, [the furs] would be used to make patterns with. Patterned trimmings…. The legs from the fall or summer caribou would be used for boots.

May Algona, 1999

The skins with thin hair were used for hats too. On some parts of the hat, the hair would be shaved off. Some had black hair and some red, and would have a loon beak on the front. That is what Inuit used a long time ago. They used caribou skins any way they could a long time ago. The white breast part of the caribou would be used for designs on dark fur.

Archie Komak, 1998

[The calves'] furs would become darker as they are growing. When they are unborn, their furs are red. We wait until August to hunt caribou because the fur is better then…. The Inuit would try to catch them when the furs from the calves and cows are good enough for clothing. When the furs get nice, the people would split up. They would be together during the spring until the caribou furs are ready. When people wanted clothing, they would go hunting. When the furs are ready for use for warm clothing, they do not shed as much.

Mackie Kaosoni, 1998

[Qitirmiut] would call [the caribou] *kan'ngalaq* because they would be losing their fur. And in the summer they would be called *haggaruq*, because their fur is good enough for clothing. That is when they are in the summer. Then they would be called *ukiuliqmik* in the fall when their fur was thickest, good enough for clothing.

Nellie Hikok, 1999

I had needles made from bones, not the ones white people make. I have seen needles that my mom and dad used. They were made from caribou antlers, copper, and they were made for different purposes. *Qainnijjut*—bone needles.

Lena Kamoayok, 1998

The [caribou thigh] bone where you have marrow from, they used them for needles also.

Annie Komak, 1998

Caribou skins are warm for bedding when you have to overnight. For travellers, they are the best because they are warmer and do not collect moisture.

Lena Kamoayok, 1998

You know when caribou get really fat? [Inuit] hammer the tallow to make oil for heating lamps.

Annie Komak, 1998

When people cut themselves, they would use the outer covering of the heart as a bandage.... [It] was dried up and used as a bandage ... because it does not leak.

Mabel Angulalik, 1998

They used caribou skins for water buckets and the handles for carrying. The fur is removed when it is to be used for strings. They used them for sleds and strings. They would cut the caribou skins and remove the hair to make ropes. They would soak the skin until the fur peels off, then make ropes from it.

Annie Komak, 1998

[Caribou skins] were made into dog harnesses and even to cover dog teats.... Caribou skins were used to cover the sleds. This protected whatever was on the sled [so it] did not get broken during travels.

Lena Kamoayok, 1998

Caribou skins, they even used them for sliding down hills!

Annie Komak, 1998

Even though skidoos are used, caribou skins should not be forgotten nowadays. If skidoos break down, they can use the skins for sleds.... Anything that is traditionally made should not be forgotten. Never leave [home] without them.

John Akana, 1998

Medicinal Purposes

In the past, some parts of the caribou were used for medicinal purposes. Fat from the neck of a caribou was used for soap, sometimes to clean a wound. Lymph nodes from the neck were used as medicine.

In traditional times, late summer or early fall skins without fur were also used to make kayaks for the following spring. These were made by soaking the hides, removing the fur, sewing the skins together, and stretching the skin around a wooden (usually spruce) frame. Willow was used for the ribs. By similar means, skins were also used to make drums. Caribou skins wrapped around wood were used to beat the drums.

> The [caribou] skin would go inside the kayak, because they are narrow. They were made to go smoothly in the water and to fit you as well. We would fill in the front and back and the top with whatever it could hold.
>
> *George Kuptana, 1998*

Tools and Hunting Equipment

Caribou antlers and bones could be split and carved into implements such as bows, arrows, scrapers, drills, and knives. The shoulder blades from caribou are good for making into scrapers for skins. With scrapers, knives, and other tools, a little bit of copper was often tied to the bone with sinew.

> Making bows and arrows…. Caribou antlers, you got to make them thin so they do not bend. So they will not break, you cook them and boil them…. Before you cool it off, these two bones, and these caribou horns, you stick them in the earth….They would stick them in moss to cool faster….They do not let them air-cool. They are cooled off quicker in order to make them bend, strengthening them.
>
> *Jack Alonak, 1998*

> I remember seeing my grandfather using a bow and arrow….When I was younger, it was fun to use a bow and arrow….It was even better than the white people's bow. I do not like the white people's bow and arrow; the arrow is not as strong.
>
> *George Kuptana, 1998*

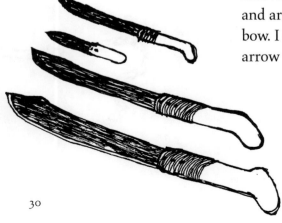

Caribou antlers are used for bows. Tendons [sinew] are used on the bows as well.... Caribou tendons are braided and used.

Bessie Omilgoitok, 1998

The antlers are used for ... spearheads. They are used for fishing. There would be sort of like barbs in between the antlers. They are called *nuiyaaqpak*. The other is a *kakivak* [fish spear].

Paul Omilgoitok, 1998

[Inuit] had drying racks as well, used for drying clothing over the stone lamp. We would make tea as well using the lamp. It tasted better when we used caribou tallow for fuelling the stone lamp. Some of the drying racks were big [one-half metre by one-quarter metre]. They were made of caribou antlers in a circular shape and used as hangers.

May Algona, 1999

Caribou and muskox ribs were used as bows and drills. Caribou kneecaps were used as mouthpieces when using the drill.

Lena Kamoayok, 1998

JACK ALONAK AT THE ELDERS' CENTRE WORKSHOP, KUGLUKTUK, 1999.

During the spring, summer, and fall, Qitirmiut made tents by sewing caribou hides together and supporting them in the middle with a pole made of driftwood or long willow or alder branches, especially from shorelines. Sometimes, fish spears or harpoon shafts doubled as tent poles.

Tents were secured by seal or caribou skin ropes or by stones around the base. A ring of stones remained when the tent was taken down. These rings can still be seen today, scattered throughout the land, and mark places where Qitirmiut once gathered to hunt, fish, or visit friends and family. Dozens of rings clustered together are often found where two rivers meet, where the fishing or sealing is good, or along rivers at caribou crossing places. Old tent rings clustered together and scattered bones mark places where families met as a large group, whereas single tent rings indicate places where people lived for a brief period.

In the fall time, in September, we would hunt caribou to be used as tents and bedding, preparing meat for the winter, stocking up on tallow. It would rain outside when we were trying to dry caribou skins. Then you would wish you were in a tent. Tents were made even when the caribou skins were still damp.... Canvas tents are not so warm in September. When the caribou skin tent was done, boy was it ever warm! It would be just like being in a house once the tent was done.... A lot of people had caribou skin tents, as well as bedding. There was no other material except caribou.

May Algona, 1999

Since the 1950s, Qitirmiut have mainly used square (or rectangular) canvas tents. One way to tell the difference between old and new campsites is to look at whether stones mark out squares or ovals and circles. Another way is to see how deeply the rocks have sunk into the tundra. Small fire rings inside the circles of stones are a sign that a camp is very old. One can barely make out the circles at some ancient sites. Many sites continue to be used today as they were in the past. Such sites show remains from both kinds of tents.

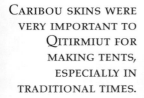

CARIBOU SKINS WERE VERY IMPORTANT TO QITIRMIUT FOR MAKING TENTS, ESPECIALLY IN TRADITIONAL TIMES.

Besides the skin and bones, caribou innards were also used. For example, the stomach of the caribou was often used to carry blood from the hunting site back to the camp to mix with broth for blood soup.

> The esophagus of the caribou was used for storing caribou tallow. When the tallow cooled, it was poured in.
>
> *Lena Kamoayok, 1998*

> When a woman adopted and did not have any milk to nurse the baby, she would use caribou milk. They also used [blood] soup for feeding the baby.
>
> *Annie Komak, 1998*

> Inuit who grew up on [blood] soup drink it more and crave it more.
>
> *Lena Kamoayok, 1998*

> They would make bottles out of the thin area of skin from a caribou. Yeah, they would blow it up, tie it, and dry it up, just like a little bottle. And nipples too.
>
> *Jack Alonak, 1998*

> [Qitirmiut] used Arctic cotton to make strings and dipped them into caribou tallow to make candles.
>
> *Annie Komak, 1998*

In the past, caribou were critically important to Qitirmiut for food, clothing, tools, shelter, kayaks, and in other ways that made survival possible. During the past few decades, most Qitirmiut have settled in communities and are not as dependent on caribou. Yet caribou continue to be important to Qitirmiut culture, identity, and subsistence. A unique tie to the past, they remind people of their ancestors who suffered during the times when the caribou failed to come. As in traditional times, activities around caribou such as hunting, butchering, and making caribou clothing help to define what it is to be an Inuk. Indeed, to practise these activities is to weave the fabric of Qitirmiut culture that links elders and youth.

2 The Seasonal Round

The way that Qitirmiut and caribou interact has always changed with each season. In traditional times, Qitirmiut travel routes paralleled the caribou migrations, as people moved from one camp to another throughout the year (see MAP 2, PAGE 9). Today, depending on the time of year, caribou are still often the reason for people's camps and travels.

The spring migration north, the summer calving period, the fall rut, and the caribou's winter migration south form part of an annual cycle that links Qitirmiut and caribou. Changes in the nature and activity of wildlife and in the weather are tied to the phases of the moon and together define six seasons in a year.

> We did not have calendars back then. [Inuit] used the moon only.... They used the moon as a way to tell seasons long ago. When the moon would come during the spring thaw, when there is water, the caribou are calving and the birds are nesting. That is how it was used.... The moon would go away again during the month of June. When it returns you know when the birds are moulting ... which is during the month of July. The moon was the only way the Inuit knew the time of the year.... We did not know it was July then. After it disappeared, it would return and then it would be August. That is when the caribou furs would get nice.... The birds would be flying again. The young birds would have grown then. That is how they knew the seasons.
>
> *Frank Analok, 1999*

Changes in local wildlife, weather, and the moon are signals that inform where people choose to hunt, camp, and travel. People's campsites and travel routes are often the same ones used by their ancestors, who also relied on their acute observations of the animals, the weather, and the moon. Many of the routes are also different now that the majority of Qitirmiut do not live inland any more.

TRAVELLING WITH THE CARIBOU

Qitirmiut used to travel with the caribou through the seasons, but this has changed today. There were many arduous challenges in moving with the caribou. Some women told of having to give birth one day, the newborn "caught in a caribou skin," and packing the baby on their back the very next day while walking or sledding to a new camp. A few men recalled carrying heavy caribou skin tents and other camp materials for long distances across the tundra. Walking overland in the summer was more difficult than riding on a sled in the winter.

Since the establishment of the trading posts, Qitirmiut have generally spent the summers along the coast and the winters inland. During the spring migration, people followed the caribou northwards. Come fall, Qitirmiut followed the caribou southwards as they returned to their wintering grounds.

Upin'ngakhaq (early spring) has always brought great happiness. With the warmer sun and longer days comes the return of animals and birds from their southern wintering grounds. Upin'ngakhaq has always been tied to caribou migration and a bounty of meat after a winter of relative scarcity.

Today, starting in the early part of May, going to the cabins or tents to hunt the migrating caribou is fun. Here, one can watch as yearlings and pregnant cows lead the way northwards to the calving grounds. A few weeks later, the bulls follow. In traditional times, Qitirmiut families travelled to meet with large groups in common camps nearby their caribou hunting grounds.

> People would gather in the spring when the caribou
> would migrate inland. They have always hunted there.
> It is their land and they know it well, even before the
> white people came.
>
> *John Akana, 1998*

> Most people lived where the caribou were plentiful.
> There were hardly any people living by the ocean
> because there were no caribou, nothing at all. The cari-
> bou were inland only; there would be people anywhere
> inland from Tahiryoak. The people would winter
> inland where the caribou were. During the spring,
> around April, people would head to the ocean. There
> was a lot of people inland.
>
> *May Algona, 1999*

> That is Hingik, where we used to spend our springs.…
> There are many old campsites there.… We would
> only spend the spring there to make dry meat.…
> Also at Hanningayuk, I had camps there during the
> summer and winter.… Also around Tahiryoak.
>
> *Jessie Hagialok, 1998*

As spring advances, the long hours and warm temperatures make it easier and more pleasurable to both hunt caribou and prepare *mipku* (dry meat).

> My parents would hunt caribou in the spring for
> drying, when there are no flies.
>
> *Frank Analok, 1998*

As *upin'ngaaq* (late spring) arrives, hunters are more selective because they know that the caribou will be migrating for several weeks. Hunters look for caribou that are the healthiest or the fattest, although one cannot be too fussy. One hunter told of the time he went out hunting for the day and within half an hour saw a caribou. The caribou was small and rather skinny, so he decided to leave it. Much to his dismay, he did not see another caribou for the next twelve hours of hunting. He explained that he had been too fussy.

One must watch the *nuna* (land) and the sea ice closely so that once the ice melts and travelling over the land becomes difficult, one can start using boats to hunt caribou. Today, going by boat to look for caribou on the islands in Bathurst Inlet during *auyaq* (summer) is a fun way to hunt compared to hunting inland and fighting off all the bugs.

Narrow places along a river where caribou are likely to swim across are called *nalluit*. In the olden days, people would hunt by kayak and use spears while on the water. On the land, they used bows and arrows.

During the spring and summer they [Inuit] come back
to their campgrounds that are near caribou crossings.…
The narrow parts are where they catch fish.

Annie Komak, 1998

This is where I have heard people talk about caribou
crossings. Back then, it was just like people had rifles
because they caught so many here. They used kayaks.

Nellie Hikok, 1999

They used a kayak for hunting caribou that are swimming. The *inukhuit* [stone markers] were used. It was a
necessity when they hunted without rifles. All they
had were bows and arrows.

Mabel Angulalik, 1998

When [caribou] are crossing the main route, there is
always hair on the river. Along the shore, just along the
Burnside River. See balls of hair, bunch of balls. There are
balls of hair along the river, along the whole Burnside.

George Kapolak Haniliak, 1998

The Dawn of a New Spring

Spring is here! The first geese have returned, their wings cutting through the still cool air like your knife cuts through snow when making blocks for an iglu. With the geese and cranes finally overhead, you know that the caribou will not be far behind.

Imagine crouching strategically behind a hunting blind made of rocks, warm in your caribou skin pants, parka, and *kamngit* (boots), and waiting patiently for the first caribou to come close. You look over at your brothers, uncles, cousins, and father, who hide behind a rocky outcrop nearby. These men are hunched over, curved backs like boulders and camouflaged perfectly in their weathered caribou skin clothing that fades into the brown hues of the parched spring tundra and gravel. They wait without weariness, their bows and arrows ready. Meanwhile, your sisters, aunts, and kids are off in the distance, moving methodically and deliberately to steer the caribou towards you. It is a joyous time and the excitement builds quietly. The caribou are here! The caribou are here! Let them walk to the waiting hunters.

At last, the caribou are funnelled towards you. The thunder of hooves shakes the tundra as you launch arrows from your hiding place, all the while shooting accurately but quickly. You are careful to aim for the neck, so that the kill is fast and less painful. Sometimes you wait for two caribou to be side by side so that one arrow will hit fatally both animals. Your heart races as you hunt as many caribou as you need: one, two, three …

For the hours following the last caribou that passes, you skin and butcher the carcasses to be packed back to nearby caches or camp, where the women will cut the meat and prepare the skins. Spring has arrived, the feeling is festive, and the caribou are back: once again, you can feed your family. This year, you will not starve. The caribou have come.

—*Researchers' Notes,*
Hiukkittaak Elder-Youth Camp, August 1998

Since it can be hot and the mosquitoes and flies become pests in the summer, people hunt less and fish more than in other seasons. As in the past, early summer is a good time for catching fish and making *piffi*, or dry fish, for the coming winter while enjoying the cooler and windier air along the coast. In contrast, hunting on the land in the summer is a challenge, because the meat has to be packed back to camp while one walks through thick clouds of bugs. During the Hiukkittaak Elder-Youth Camp, caribou was cut up so it could be folded tightly into a suitcase and carried on people's backs more easily.

> Sometimes people would stop hunting, usually in July when the weather gets too hot.... People would stop hunting during the month of July, because of the worms. In August they would store or cache meat.
>
> *Charlie Keyok, 1998*

> We would hunt less when there are flies, as the worms would spoil the meat. Every August, when the fur gets nice to use for clothing and the meat will not spoil, they would hunt again.
>
> *George Kuptana, 1998*

> Hunting caribou in July? Too many mosquitoes!
>
> *Moses Koihok, 1998*

EARLY FALL   Hunting resumes in *ukiakhaq* (early fall) because it is cool enough that the meat does not spoil and the fur is good for clothing. During the summer, warble fly larvae burrow out from under the caribou fur and create tears in the hide that look like bullet holes. A skin with these holes is not very good for clothing, bedding, drums, kayaks, tents, or other uses.

Ukiakhaq is a good time for hunting because the caribou, particularly the bulls, are the fattest and healthiest after a summer of grazing and storing fat on the rump (known as backfat). If the summer has not been too hot the backfat can be more than eight centimetres thick, making the bulls appear to have small tails. Thick backfat is one sign of a prime bull.

The bulls would get real fat during the fall.... When the meat of the [caribou] has been cached ... they are really good for eating. We would eat more frozen meat. During late summer the yearlings would get beautiful and they would be hunted most for clothing, inner parkas. The bull skins would be used for bedding as well as tents. There were lots for bedding, large tents as well. People would catch a lot of caribou.

May Algona, 1999

ANNIE KOMAK, HIUKKITTAAK
ELDER-YOUTH CAMP, 1998.

Usually in the ... early fall I usually go for the bulls, 'cause they have more fat, more meat, for dry meat in the fall. The hides are good too.

Allen Kapolak, 1998

Unlike the spring, when hunger and the desire for new foods were the driving forces behind the hunt, *ukiaq* (late fall) is when Qitirmiut planned ahead to cache enough meat to last the long winter.

LATE FALL

People used to pile up a lot of skins for future use in case there were not any caribou the following year.

Lena Kamoayok, 1998

They used to make piles and piles of skins for next year's use. For future use because maybe the next year there will not be any caribou.

Annie Komak, 1998

Today, one way to plan ahead is to bring much more food and heating fuel than necessary for a short trip. In the past, to plan for the future meant to put away stores of meat in stone caches at popular campsites or along typical travel routes.

When people hunted for the winter back then they were hardly home. I was like that myself. They would be quite a ways from camp. Hunting to stock up on tallow, caching meat for the winter. They would try to get enough to last them the winter. Stocking up on skins, meat, taking the whole caribou. When we were not cutting up and preparing caribou, it was fun watching hunters, but we would have to haul [the caribou meat] as well.

Nellie Hikok, 1999

On the land, down by Hanningayuk and Tahiryoak, in their wintering grounds, they would bury food to use in the winter and for the dogs as well. They still hunt for caribou in Umingmaktuuk. They would catch five, six, or nine to make dry meat.

Charlie Keyok, 1998

In the past, just before the first snow was a good time to store meat in stone caches. By then the flies were gone and the temperatures were cool enough to keep the meat from becoming rancid under the stones. These caches can still be seen almost everywhere, especially near high points on rocky outcrops, along caribou migration routes, and at caribou river crossings.

Sometimes caribou meat was cached, when there is no chance of the meat being spoiled by worms and heat. When the weather starts cooling off, maybe in August, they would cache meat for later when there was less food. Nothing went to waste. Whatever was not needed right away was cached or stored. That is the way it used to be back then.

Mabel Angulalik, 1998

MAY ALGONA,
KUGLUKTUK, 1999.

When they are heading north in the fall, people would put away food for use later on, digging in the ground, wrapping the meat in the skins and burying it … just like a freezer, deep-freezer. People would boil [meat] for eating when there were not any caribou around.

May Algona, 1999

I remember walking from Kapihiliktuuk [Hope Bay] to Qalgiliq…. In the fall time we came down by this river to our outpost camps. From there, from Kaphiiliktuuk, is where we would stop while travelling inland during the fall.

Annie Komak, 1998

During the fall they would stay down there [inland]. They would start travelling from [Hiukkittaak River] and hunt or fish along the way. They did not depend on the white people for help then. They would spend the summer along the river and during freeze-up they would start travelling down that way…. That is how they lived back then. They had to find food to survive. It seemed like they never got tired.

Mary Kaniak, 1998

USUALLY AROUND THE TIME WHEN THE RUT BEGAN, QITIRMIUT STARTED TO TRAVEL WITH THE CARIBOU AS THEY MOVED SOUTHWARDS TO THEIR WINTERING GROUNDS.

WINTER

At this time, Qitirmiut followed the herd inland in search of caribou that would be grazing where the new snow was still thin enough for them to paw through for food. Once the caribou migrated out of the region, people subsisted on fish and small game, along with cached caribou, until the spring migration.

Qitirmiut usually went to different places during the *ukiuq* (winter), which varied for each family or group of families. People would camp where the trapping, fishing, or seal hunting could carry them through the winter. Today, ukiuq is not as tough as in the past, because store-bought food is available. Nobody starves to death any more unless they get caught out on the land or the sea ice in a storm and cannot be rescued because of bad weather.

When trapping and fur trading were introduced, Qitirmiut camped where there was an abundance of fur-bearers. The men would set up a camp for their families and then leave for long periods—trapping, hunting, or travelling to the trading posts. Women experienced loneliness and hardships when their husbands and other family members were gone.

I left my family at this base camp and stayed away for about nine days…. [It was] around here, near the place where our first child died. They called it Beechey Lake [Hanningayuk]. People used to camp there during the

springtime. Inuit used to travel from the coast and spend the winter there because there was a lot of game to hunt.

George Kuptana, 1997

In the wintertime, the people go to the ocean to hunt seals and fish for cod. That is where they would stay during the winter, the people long ago…. They would get stones to make seal oil lamps to keep warm in the winter during their stay inland while hunting and fishing.

John Akana, 1998

They would cache food to last the winter. They bought necessities such as tea and kerosene in those days…. People would offer us food while we waited. The men would catch enough food for their wives before leaving them at camps.

Mary Kaniak, 1998

Long ago, Inuit did not have rifles. They stayed at their traditional camps inland, further inland than here…. The Inuit then started using traps and rifles at their traditional hunting grounds, more after the post on the coast opened. Shortly after that, the company [Hudson's Bay Company] began buying skins. So after the freeze-up, the inland people would travel down to trade the skins they had caught…. The Inuit would come down by dog team to trade and then return to their traditional camps further in the Barren Lands. Since they started to own rifles, they started trapping all the way down to the coast. Shortly after that, the inland people, as they were called, settled along the coast to trap.

John Akana, 1998

TABLE 2
Inuinnaqtun Names for the Seasons

Through the six seasons of the year, Qitirmiut travelled and camped along caribou migration routes.

Inuinnaqtun
  English

Upin'ngakhaq
  Early Spring
  March–April

Upin'ngaaq
  Late Spring
  May–June

Auyaq
  Summer
  July–August

Ukiakhaq
  Early Fall
  August–September

Ukiaq
  Late Fall
  October–November

Ukiuq
  Winter
  December–February

Qitirmiut have always relied on their observations of the weather, the moon, and wildlife activity to forecast where and when caribou could be found. Throughout the upin'ngakhaq and upin'ngaaq, Qitirmiut awaited the arrival of the caribou en route to their calving grounds. Auyaq, ukiakhaq, and ukiaq were times to hunt large bulls and cache meat for the long winter ahead. Come ukiuq, when the caribou had returned to their southern wintering grounds, people fished while waiting for the caribou to return. The seasonal round of Qitirmiut was intrinsically linked to the seasonal movements of the caribou.

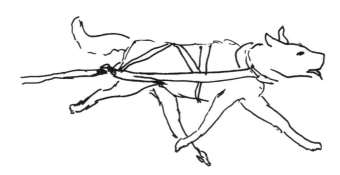

3 Harvesting Caribou

The caribou harvest includes hunting, butchering, preparing, and cooking caribou meat as well as all of the traditions that surround these activities. Each activity flows into the next and may be either carried out by one person or handed from one person to another. In any case, people like to work together to share in the important task of harvesting caribou for their communties.

There are many ways to hunt caribou. To hunt, one has to show respect and get inside the head of a caribou to understand how a caribou feeds, moves, sees, hears, and smells.

> When the people were watching the caribou, it would
> seem like they are part of the caribou.
>
> *Nellie Hikok, 1999*

If there is snow, one must look for tracks that lead to the caribou. While looking for tracks, one has to think like a caribou to know where they might go or otherwise anticipate their behaviour. MAP 3 (PAGE 177) shows some typical hunting grounds used by Qitirmiut.

> In the olden days, they used to try to figure out where
> the migration pattern was going. They would have
> their camp set up where they could easily ambush the
> caribou on their route, on their migration route to the
> calving grounds.
>
> *Naikak Hakongak, 1998*

> I went out hunting with a few of the elders before, when
> I just started going out. That time we used to have to go
> ninety miles to get a caribou, and my uncle used to shoot
> the leader first and then shoot the rest when there is not
> too many. Because the caribou follow the leader, when
> the caribou leader stops, the rest of them stop.
>
> *George Kavanna, 1999*

Many traditional strategies have been passed down and are in use today. For example, it is commonly known that you should stand downwind so the caribou cannot smell you, stay still or move slowly so the caribou cannot see you, and tread and talk quietly so the caribou cannot hear you.

Nowadays we have Sorels [commercial boots] and they make lots of noise [on the snow]. Caribou mukluks are much quieter. They make it easier to sneak up on caribou.

Naikak Hakongak, 2000

Learning to think like a caribou comes from spending years and years watching caribou. Starting as a young child, a person learns how to spot a caribou, then patiently observe and study it for a period of time. Taking time to watch caribou move, eat, rest, and mingle gives one a chance to start thinking like a caribou—predicting where the caribou will go next and, finally, hunting the animal.

We would look for fresh caribou tracks. We would follow the fresh caribou tracks. They are not seen in the summer, only on trails. In the winter we would hunt caribou when we spotted fresh tracks. That is how we would get to the caribou.

Charlie Keyok, 1998

People would hunt caribou by dog teams. They took care of their dogs, trying to keep them quiet. They would get close to the caribou on either side, and the dogs did not go after the caribou. They would be careful not to make any noises.

Moses Koihok, 1998

In the past, hunting techniques included using handmade spears and bows and arrows. Stone *talut* and inukhuit were used, especially at river crossings or along migration routes, to steer caribou towards waiting hunters who were hiding behind blinds. Women and children would sometimes yell and chase the caribou towards the hunters too. Many inukhuit and talut remain standing today across the land.

HUNTING
TECHNIQUES

There would be many landmarks in place over a long stretch.... My parents would tell stories about using bows and arrows and landmarks. They would pile rocks to look like people. They would use landmarks to move the caribou to the direction of the hunters hiding behind blinds. They would use kayaks too. I have seen that at a caribou water crossing before.... I used to ride on [a kayak] on my belly. I would be lying down. I would try not to lift my head up.... There are still quite a few hunting blinds ... you might still see all those rocks standing. Those are all to drive the caribou. Nowadays we do not need those. We use rifles.

Charlie Keyok, 1998

[When Inuit hunted caribou by kayak] they would
pull them with a rope. They would knot it … and pull
[the caribou] to the area where they would bury it or
by the tent where they would make dry meat. People
used to travel in kayaks, hunting on the land, carrying
their kayaks because they were light.… A bow and
arrow is more difficult to use than [a spear in] the
kayak. I learned to use the kayak … from my grandfather. He made me one. You have to be careful though
how much meat you carry on the kayak: you have to
keep in mind how much the kayak can carry. The bow
and arrow was more difficult to use, although they
were fun to use, and you were sure for a catch.
Sometimes you would catch nothing though. I found
them difficult to use. Others handled them very well in
the olden days. That is what they have always used for
hunting. There were rifles then, but we would shoot for
fun with the bow and arrow.

George Kuptana, 1998

In the past, communication between people during the hunt was important.
Especially during the spring migration, Qitirmiut had to announce the arrival
of the caribou. Hunting efforts were more successful when people spread out
and distracted the caribou by making noises and frightening the caribou
towards a waiting hunter.

When people were expecting caribou, they would all
scatter. They would scatter and wait for caribou to
come.… When a [man] was looking out for caribou
and spotted them first, he would let others know by
making a fire showing off thick smoke. Everyone
would go towards him happily. That was when a person would first spot caribou.… It would be a happy
time when we saw that smoke!

May Algona, 1999

CHANGING WAYS   Caribou hunting techniques today are very different from those of the past. Whereas bows and arrows, skin kayaks, and stone blinds and markers used to be common, nowadays rifles are used. It is easy for people to track or find caribou by using snowmobiles, powerboats, airplanes, and all-terrain vehicles. Although herd migrations may have changed, modern technology has also made it easier for people to adapt to such changes. In many ways, the departure from traditional hunting techniques has altered the relationship between Qitirmiut and caribou.

It is not as it used to be in the past. People worked hard then, suffering sometimes, beyond their ability. Nowadays, people do not work as hard when they are hunting. They do not have to walk long distances; they can just sit and hunt. Today they have rifles and scopes, so it is not as hard to hunt.

Frank Analok, 1998

They never caught a lot [of caribou] because they did not have rifles then.... They do not catch too many caribou nowadays because they have guidelines. There are stores now.

Mabel Angulalik, 1998

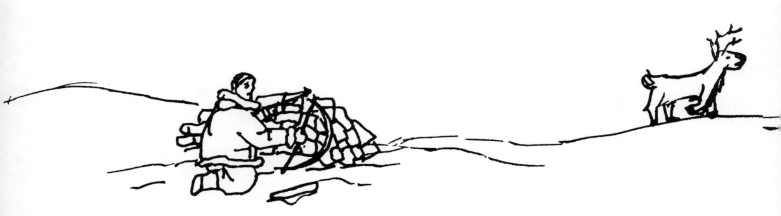

I grew up when rifles were already in use. There was hardly any ammunition then and hunting was their only job. Sometimes [Inuit] would make ammunition with whatever they had using the same shell. We did not know then that they would be plentiful.

George Kuptana, 1998

Every August people would hunt relentlessly for caribou to be used as clothing. The thin fur. Nowadays it seems people do not know how to work with them [caribou skins].

Bessie Omilgoitok, 1998

I used to go around visiting other camps, anywhere with a dog team. Now there are a truck and a skidoo. When I was younger I had a six-dog dog team. When I was younger, when I started travelling around, I used to go around visiting anywhere down that way around Hanningayuk.… Even to Tahikyoak! I went visiting other camps on a dog team. There were not any vehicles then, none at all.

Archie Komak, 1998

Qitirmiut still rely on caribou as a source of food, which can be a problem when the caribou migration routes are many kilometres away. Hunting caribou that are far from communities can cause hardship because of the high costs of gasoline, ammunition, and food, as well as because of the time needed for a caribou-hunting trip. Many Qitirmiut say that when hunters harvest an abundance of caribou, they should give the meat to others, particularly elders. In this way, everybody remains tied to the land and the legacy of sharing and caring for one another.

Boys and girls learn to hunt early by listening to and applying lessons taught by elders and experienced hunters. In addition, they make their own observations of caribou, which continue to inform how they understand caribou throughout their lives.

When you reach fourteen, fifteen, sixteen, that is when you start hunting, that is when you get to understand and learn to hunt…. That is the age you are stronger and more energetic. That is how it is nowadays. When you reach thirteen, fourteen, teenage girls and boys learn to do things, even to this day.

Moses Koihok, 1998

The last time I watched a big migration was when I was about seven years old and we were living in Bay Chimo. I sat on top of a hill and this caribou herd was coming towards the houses. So my two older brothers and I went on a dog team and went towards where the caribou were. We sat on top of a hill and watched them. They just picked off [hunted] a couple and then the snow hook came out of the snow. My older brother, Allen, was sitting on the sled when that happened and he could not get it back in the snow. He just disappeared into the caribou herd. The dogs went

PAUL OMILGOITOK,
HIUKKITTAAK ELDER-
YOUTH CAMP, 1998.

right into the caribou herd. The caribou [grouping]
just sort of split and it seemed like nothing was going
to stop them.... From what I remember, there must
have been a good three thousand animals in the herd.

Naikak Hakongak, 1998

When I was a child, my father made me stab a calf,
close by Kuugyuak [Perry River].... [I stabbed it with]
Piruana's pocket knife. I chased the calf and stabbed it.

Bessie Angulalik, 1998

You listen to your dad closely and not stay away from him
too long. Learn everything from your dad. If he is a very
good hunter, he usually passes it on to the younger generation, sons, daughters. Paying attention is more important. I grew up with hunting. I have always hunted all
my life. First caribou I shot was when I was four years
old. And, I guess a yearling caribou, yearling, took me
over an hour to skin it out but I did it anyway. I cheated
on my boy, I helped him out, helped him skin his first
caribou. He was four years old also. His was a big bull.
Mine was a yearling.

Bobby Algona, 1999

Teaching Youth How to Hunt

Lena Kamoayok wakes at her usual time (4:00 A.M.) and prepares her teaching props. She squats in the gentle light and, with her army knife, she expertly slices through the Frosted Flakes box, carefully tracing the outline of a caribou. Within minutes she produces a target. Today, youth will learn how to hunt with the bow and arrows, crafted last month and sitting in a sacred box in her *tupiq*, or tent. When the youth awake several hours later, Lena scarcely lets them finish breakfast before she wanders up the hill towards the talut. Silently she beckons the eager students to her outdoor classroom. Here they learn to hunt caribou at the same place as their ancestors.

—Researchers' Notes,
Hiukkittaak Elder-Youth Camp, August 1998

For generations, the thunder of thousands of hooves has echoed across the tundra and alerted Qitirmiut hunters to a bounty that would provide food, clothing, and tools for survival. The simple fact that Qitirmiut would have perished without caribou led them to perfect the art of hunting, beginning with dog teams and bows and arrows and continuing with snowmobiles and rifles. Though the ways in which caribou are harvested have changed, the importance of caribou hunting to Qitirmiut identity, culture, and health continues to be profound.

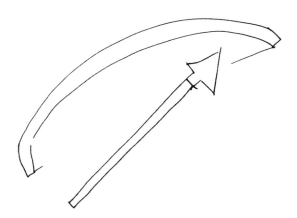

4 Preparing and Cooking Caribou

There are various ways to skin, butcher, prepare, and cook harvested caribou. Which way is used depends on where you are from, how you were taught, or the purpose for the skin and meat. Inuit from other regions of Nunavut have very different ways of skinning and butchering. Even people in different families or communities within the Bathurst Inlet region have distinct methods. For example, one hunter might start skinning the caribou from the legs, whereas another hunter might start from under the chin. These different techniques are taught to younger generations through demonstration and instruction.

The hide of the caribou changes in texture, thickness, strength, and colour with each season, and thus Qitirmiut alter how they use the skin. When they are not butchering caribou to save the skin, people follow the cutting lines they have been taught.

> The hide has lines visible to the eye that show where cuts should begin, meet, and end.
>
> *Naikak Hakongak, 2000*

> Skin from legs to legs. Start from here to the back, then to the legs. Then the head. Does not matter if you do the front legs first or the back legs first. On the leg, you start from around here, the chest. You go down from the neck down to the tail. After the legs, you turn it over and do the same thing. Cut the meat up. Take the skin off first and cut the meat up. Cut up the legs, the hindquarters to make it lighter, and the head.... You take the skin off, take the guts out, and cut it up. First the caribou leg ... you take the guts out ... first from the back, inside behind the guts.... Pull it out this way and it comes off. You cut the diaphragm right on the edge here and take it off.... I take it out with the esophagus. It comes right out. Sometimes we leave it in the winter when it's so cold out. Just cut it off and pull the lungs out.
>
> *Doris Kingnektak, 1998*

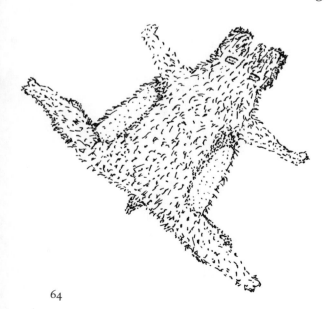

I usually start with the front leg. Just start with the front leg and just cut it right off where you could see … *nukik* [the tendon]…. Just the shoulder blade … start off, with that part and leave it all attached to the hoof. From the shoulder blade right to the hoof leave it all attached and just cut it right off. I just start at the back leg of the side that I did the front leg from. I would start with the front leg first, get the shoulder blade off, and then start with the back, the hindquarter, and get that off, and then the back strap. I would turn it over and start over the same way with the other side of the caribou. Same thing as the other side that I just did. I usually start with the front legs to cut it up and make it into dry meat. I cut the shoulder blade off right off the leg, and I would make that into dry meat, and then I would use the top bone in between the shoulder blade and the front leg. The [leg] one with just the bone marrow, use that for making boiled caribou. Then I would start off with the back strap too.

Anonymous C, 1998

I find [the bulls] are really hard to skin, summertime. In this fall weather, I do not mind. But summertime, I have noticed they are hard to skin. Must be too hot. Warm. Like you are pulling harder all the time….
I find it is much easier to skin in winter, but summertime just like they have got some kind of Krazy Glue. Some people I have noticed summertime, like my brother-in-law, I went out with him, he was cutting it up with his knife. We usually just pull it, but kind of hard to pull, and you are cutting all the time, using your pocket knife.

George Kavanna, 1999

Butchering Caribou

Learning how to butcher caribou requires patience and practice, for the techniques used depend on how the meat is going to be prepared. In the early spring and fall, *mipku* (dry meat) is popular. In the summer, caribou meat should be cooked as soon as possible because there are lots of *niviuvak* (flies). Boiled caribou and caribou stew are always popular at this time.

Caribou meat keeps people warm in the winter. In the cooler temperatures of late fall and winter, people like to eat *quaq*, frozen raw caribou, or *uuyuq*, boiled caribou. Quaq is cut into various-sized pieces and eaten frozen. An axe is used to cut off pieces of meat, which are then cut into bite-sized pieces with an *ulu* or knife. For uuyuq, the meat is cut into chunks that are thicker than those for mipku, and the marrow bones are often attached. This way of preparing caribou makes the meat tender and easy to eat. The *patiq*, marrow from the leg bones, a delicacy, is eaten using a long and skinny tool called a *haulluut* made from either a rib or the bone in the lower foreleg of a caribou. Meat from a large bull might feed thirty to forty people.

> You cannot carry the whole [caribou] to the boat so you have to cut it up. [In the winter,] when we take it home we cut it up … but when you are out, you do not cut it up, otherwise it might fall all over [off the sled].… Sometimes I cut it up. It all depends on how cold you are. If you want to take it home, the whole thing, you can warm up and cut it up later on.
>
> *Doris Kingnektak, 1998*

It is really hot right now [July], and if [my husband] goes hunting and if he gets caribou, then we put it in the freezer right now or make dry meat. We ... check it every couple of hours, turn it over and make sure there are no flies.

Anonymous C, 1998

Mipku continues to be a favourite way to prepare caribou regardless of the time of year. Mipku is made from caribou meat that is cut into thin slabs, strips, and pieces that are laid out on a clean rock, on bushes, or on racks in the sunlight and wind to dry. The rib cage is dried too. When you dry meat out on the land, it takes on the flavour of the fresh air and the smells of the tundra. Mipku tastes differently depending on where it has been dried and the amount of fat present. Once the meat dries, the surface becomes hard, and it becomes impossible for flies to lay their eggs on top. Making mipku in the fall is an important way to stock up on caribou for the winter.

PREPARING
DRY MEAT

If it were really still cold ... I would make it really thin. If we get caribou early in the spring when it is still cold out ... you need your mitts on all the time ... you could make your dry meat thick. But on days like this, you need to make your dry meat really thin, 'cause otherwise they get flies that make worms on them. That way you do not have worms on your meat when you make it into dry meat. That way you have meat all summer ... you could have dry meat till the fall. So you got to be careful how you prepare your

GEORGE KAVANNA,
IKALUKTUUTTIAK, 1998.

meat if you do not want it to go rotten.... Old people ... they have poor teeth and they need some soft meat to chew on. They are not young like us and they cannot chew really stiff, hard dry meat. So you do not just think of yourself when you are doing meat, you think of other people too.

Anonymous C, 1998

When it is still really cold and there is lots of water on the ice and there is snow all over, it is good if you can make dry meat then.... You got to check your dry meat every now and then. Just use a rock and scrape the fly eggs off or use an ulu or spoon to scrape it off. If somebody grabs a piece of meat you know they might have a worm without knowing it, so you got to be careful this time of year. *Qupilrukhaq* [larvae] will not hurt you. They just do not taste too good.

Anonymous C, 1998

COOKING WITH A KIKHUK

Caribou soup is the broth in which the boiled meat has been cooked. Today it is commonly made with rice and an assortment of vegetables. Seasonings and soup mixes are also used, especially if there is not much caribou fat to provide flavour. As in the past, people still make thick and tasty *qayuq*, blood soup, to make people strong and warm.

In the olden days, people used a fireplace made of rocks, a *kikhuk*, to cook caribou meat. To make a kikhuk, two rocks are placed side by side about fifteen to twenty centimetres apart, and another rock is propped upwards at the back. Next,

BOBBY ALGONA, KUGLUKTUK, 1999.

a large slab of rock is put atop these three rocks, so the structure looks like a flat roof on a house. The meat is placed atop this flat rock and cooked by a fire underneath. Willows, heather, driftwood, and whatever else is found easily on the tundra fuels the fire. Some places on the land are known for having large flat rocks that are good for making kikhuk. Today, kikhuk are used as a special treat when camping. The heart and liver are especially delicious when cooked this way.

> Sometimes I have a craving for cached meat. I would
> think about the liver.... Every time I get hungry when
> I was butchering caribou, I would make a fire and fry
> liver on a pan.
>
> *Nellie Hikok, 1999*

The flavour of caribou meat changes throughout the year, depending on what the caribou have been eating, what they have been doing, how much fat they have, and from which part of the animal the meat comes. Caribou taste like lichen or trees when they first arrive in the Bathurst Inlet area in the spring.

THE CHANGING
TASTE OF CARIBOU

> They winter down there in the treeline, and get all
> spruced up. They taste like spruce when they start to
> come back north again, springtime. Taste the trees.
> You shoot caribou, and it is like shooting down a tree
> and eating it. It tastes like spruce.... And [the meat]
> is brittle. The meat. It is healthy all right, but it is
> really easy to dry. After you cook it, you leave it sit-
> ting down for a little while, it tends to get dry really
> quick.... As they stay up north or stay up out of the
> trees a little longer ... their meat starts to change a
> little and after a while the taste is almost all gone
> already, totally different meat, just about. They spend
> the summer up north, feeding on lichen or willow up
> there, willows or baby birch or grasses up north.
>
> *Bobby Algona, 1999*

As the spring progresses and the snow melts, caribou start feeding on the fresh tundra. At this time, the caribou start to taste more like willows and birch. During the rutting time, the bull caribou meat tastes *qiurhungni*, which can be "musky," "gamey," or like "soap," "onions," "garlic," or "mayonnaise." The bulls have tough meat after the rut, not tender like that of the young calves or female caribou.

We hardly hunt bulls in the fall—mostly cows, young caribou. Whatever they can get. The bulls have a different flavour to them when they are rutting in the fall, but the other caribou we would hunt. Our ancestors ate the bull caribou, either cooked or frozen, caught in the fall. They did not mind the different flavour. Nowadays they are not eaten because of the flavour.

Frank Analok, 1998

In the fall, the bulls are kind of strong, strong meat. Strong bull caribou have strong taste like mayonnaise.

Doris Kingnektak, 1998

A few years back, I took a sports hunter out. He wanted me to cut a piece of [bull] back strap for him, so I cut him one. He wanted a little bit fried, although I told him it was rutting season.... So I fried some for him. He said, "Mmm, lots of garlic in it." I told him they are rutting, that is why the meat gets really sweet. He said, "Anyway, I will take some home with me. Can you pack the other side for me?".... I could not even have any. It was too strong for me.

George Kavanna, 1999

Texture is also part of how the meat tastes. Many elders prefer the young and tender calf meat over the tougher bull meat. Some younger people do not like to eat the calves, even though they are tender, because they feel sorry for them. Some kids are disgusted by the sight of blood.

TABLE 3
Inuinnaqtun
Words for
Preparing Caribou

Inuinnaqtun
English

Aakturniq
  Skinning caribou

Niqiliqiniq
  Butchering
  caribou meat

Ulu
  Woman's knife

Amiiyaiyuq
  Taking fur off
  caribou

Pilangniq
  Slicing
  caribou meat

Niqi
  Caribou meat

Kikhuk
  Fireplace
  made of rocks

Mipku
  Dry meat

Uuyuq
  Boiled
  caribou meat

Quaq
  Frozen raw
  caribou meat

Qayuq
  Blood soup

Nukik
  Tendon

Patiq
  Leg bone marrow

Qingnit
  Meat caches

Qiurhungni
  Taste of bull
  caribou meat
  during the rut

Niviuvak
  Flies

Qupilrukhaq
  Larvae

Butchering Out on the Land

After a successful hunt, elders Lena Kamoayok, Mary Kaniak, and Ella Paneyguk from Umingmaktuuk and Annie Komak and Bessie Omilgoitok from Ikaluktuuttiak attend to the finer details of butchering. Between laughter and smiles, the women tell stories. They show how to dry and care for the meat by cooling it. They tell how to identify different cuts, use the meat, prepare the skin, clean and dry the sinew, and recognize bad meat. They also tell the young women about how times have changed now that people do not have to depend upon hunting for survival.

Mary Kaniak remembers waiting a long time because of bad weather and high winds and in the winter during storms. People would lose a lot of weight just waiting. That is how people lived back then.

Part of surviving on the land is preparing caribou for everybody in the community to enjoy. Using a curved knife called an ulu, the women slice the meat into wedges. Thick pieces are for the elders, since it is easier for them to chew slightly raw meat. Others are thin and dry, as the younger people generally prefer. The young women must understand the importance of sharing in Inuit culture, the elders say. They must think of everybody when preparing food.

—Researchers' Notes,
Hiukkittaak Elder-Youth Camp, August 1998

[Inuit] like to eat tender meat. The unborn calves and seal pups are tender when they are cooked. They would eat the unborn calves because they are tender.

Annie Kaosoni, 1998

In the olden days, when there was a shortage of food, people would kill a pregnant cow. They would eat the unborn calf as well. They would skin and cook the meat.

Frank Analok, 1998

People eat the unborn calf, same as baby seals. It is the source of food.

Charlie Keyok, 1998

The various ways in which Qitirmiut prepare and cook caribou are specific to the Kitikmeot region in general and to each family or hunter in particular. As in the past, these ways are passed down from one generation to the next, with an emphasis on respecting caribou throughout the processes of preparing and cooking the meat. In preserving this knowledge, family members have opportunities to spend quality time together sharing in traditional ways.

5 Cultural Rules and Caribou

Elders say that the beliefs, traditions, and customs surrounding caribou ought to be followed. If you do not follow the *pitquhiit*, they say, you will not be a good hunter—or perhaps not even a good person. Many pitquhiit are also *maligaghat*, rules, in that they are absolutely necessary for the good of everybody.

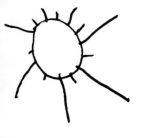

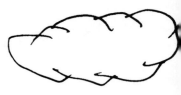

**CARIBOU SHOULD
NOT SUFFER IN DEATH**

Do not let the caribou suffer … [when] you shoot it.
You just do not let it run off. You chase after it until
you shoot it down and never let it go. That is what we
do. Even if it is ten miles away, we still go after it. Make
sure that it is not just left to suffer and die somewhere.
Like my brother when he goes hunting.… He makes sure
if he wounds a caribou, he gets it.… Except only if he does
not have enough gas or bullets to. Then you do not have
a choice and you have to make your way home too.…
If we see a wounded caribou just hobbling or just lay-
ing there without moving except just to look around,
we shoot it 'cause we know it is sick or been wounded.…
We would rather shoot it than let it suffer.

Anonymous C, 1998

We usually catch the caribou, shoot the caribou. We go
to it and if it is still alive, we kill it right away. People
used to say, "Do not let the animal suffer," so we have
to kill it right away when we get to it.… When the
caribou is still alive, you grab the antler and have a
knife and poke it right on the back of the neck. It dies
right away. Poke in the brain, here behind the neck.

Nancy Haniliak, 1998

[If somebody does not share their meat, people] would probably say, "That person cannot even share his meat!" They would say that that person should not even go out hunting since he cannot share or whatever. 'Cause everybody shares. They share their meat.

Nancy Haniliak, 1998

We send the meat out to family all the time for the ones that do not really go out and have dry meat to eat.... It is not only for us that we shoot the caribou. We always give out dry meat, pack it up and send it out and call to make sure somebody gets their meat before it gets rotten. So it is not only for us that we hunt caribou to make dry meat. It is for family all over [the region] ... [If you do not share your meat] nobody is going to like you. You are so greedy, get out of my cabin! You are not [going] to have any of mine.... I do not want to know you.

Anonymous C, 1998

If you ignore the first caribou you see and you do not shoot it, then you are not going to have good luck after that. You should not be choosy when you are out caribou hunting. That is one thing that I have heard.... The story I told earlier was that you are not supposed to just bypass the first caribou that you see, hoping to see a bigger or better one. I just bypassed that one caribou and I said we might see more today. Sure enough, we did not see any more caribou all day long, so it is. Some things are true. Especially when the caribou are not plentiful, then you try not to ignore the first you see. If you really want it, you will get it. Otherwise, if you just ignore it, you will not see any more and we did not see any more.

Naikak Hakongak, 1998

It is the same with all the other animals: they can hear you talking no matter how many miles away or if you are in the house. All animals, they listen to you talking, they hear you talking. I have heard from the old folks that one person was saying how great a hunter he was, very great hunter. He really knows how to hunt, bragging, bragging all the time, and then one day he said he was really sure of himself, he was going to get an animal, he was going to shoot a caribou, he said, "I am gonna go get a caribou from over there." So he went over there, hunted all over the place, cannot find anything.... Came back home with nothing. And people kept telling him that he should not brag about these things, other- wise the animals are going to hear you and they know, know exactly where you want to go. They are going to move away from you and nothing is going to be there. Everything is going to hide from that area.

Bobby Algona, 1999

I can remember one time my mom saying when you catch a pregnant cow in the spring you are supposed to take the foetus out and put snow in its mouth as water for the afterlife. Give it snow, put snow in its mouth for its first taste of water or something fresh other than mother's milk. Supposed to give you good hunt- ing luck too. Supposed to be able to always have good luck after that.

Naikak Hakongak, 1998

JACK ALONAK,
HIUKKITTAAK, 1998.

I believe a lot of superstitions about caribou, like for boys there are some certain rules that you could not do anything to the girls, tease the girls, fight the girls or whatever, fight with the girls. In order to be

a good hunter, you do not tease your sisters or your
younger siblings, do not fight with them, otherwise
if you do you would have a hard time hunting, if
you go out hunting.

Bobby Algona, 1999

Some pitquhiit seem to have come about in order to explain supernatural
or strange events, while other pitquhiit seem to give hope to people. During
traditional times, baby boys were valued for their strength and ability to hunt
when they grew up. Families hoped for boys and were considered fortunate if a
baby boy was born. Baby girls were seen as a burden when wildlife was scarce
or weather was especially harsh.

My grandpa used to tell me to have the nukik [ten-
dons] of the bull. I was saying, "No way I do not want
any of those".... But he was telling me that if I have
those nukiks from the certain part of the male caribou.... I would have only boys. He was telling me that
he wanted me to have them. I told him no, it does not
look too good, I do not want any of it. So he did not
force me. But it is because in the olden days the boys
were more useful than the girls. But nowadays I do
not know if it is still the same. But to me it is okay.
I do not mind having girls. I do not mind having just
one boy and three or four girls, it will not bother me.

CULTURAL BELIEFS
TO DO WITH
CARIBOU MEAT

But I guess long ago after some people used to have baby girls, I heard they just left them there to die. To them they were more work, just feed them until they get old enough and take care of them until they get old enough to go off with a man, which was also work for the old people long ago. But I guess it is okay now.… I am not passing that [not eating the meat on the caribou snout] on to my daughter too, because if she grows older and if she likes to eat it, then I will just let her have it. I liked it, and I use to eat it and I never knew about the story. The story was when you are pregnant you cannot have those because when you are about to deliver your baby, you are going to breathe really hard and have a hard time breathing. I never heard of that and it never bothered me when I was having a baby or when I had my babies, so I was okay. I guess as long as you do not know what the story is, then you should be okay.

Anonymous C, 1998

I have heard a lot of things that, because you are a boy, sometimes you eat the certain parts of the caribou. Or you are almost unlimited to what you can eat of the caribou. Whereas little girls are a little more restricted to some parts of the animal. Like cartilage or stomach contents I think is one of them.… There are some things that girls could eat, a lot of superstitions.

Bobby Algona, 1999

With modern influences, many younger Qitirmiut have not heard, do not believe, or fail to follow pitquhiit. This may be because of a changing relationship between Qitirmiut and caribou. Alternatively, it may be that some of these traditional pitquhiit have not been passed down or recorded, and so they have been lost to the culture. That young people do not speak the same language as elders or live in the old way is also a factor.

I believe that [you must not brag about being a good hunter]. Even though being the younger generation, I do not want to take chances. It is folklore, but I am not going to muddle with it.

Bobby Algona, 1999

Pitquhiit have always guided Qitirmiut in their interactions with caribou so as to ensure respect for caribou and to give hope, provide luck, or explain natural events. These cultural rules encompass the beliefs, traditions, and customs that ought to be followed. Many pitquhiit are also considered maligaghat, rules that must be adhered to because they are necessary for the good of everybody. Although some of these cultural rules have been lost over time, the remaining conventions that form part of a caribou code are central to the relationship between Qitirmiut and caribou.

6 Herds of the Kitikmeot

Qitirmiut hunt several different "kinds" of caribou. One herd, which biologists distinguish as the Bathurst and the Queen Maud caribou, is collectively known to Qitirmiut as *Ahiarmiut,* or the Mainland or Barrenland caribou herd. Most elders and hunters do not distinguish between different herds of Ahiarmiut. Another herd, the *Kiillinik,* Victoria Island caribou, spends the winters on the mainland and migrates to Kiillinik for the summers. Ahiarmiut caribou are larger and darker than the smaller and whiter Kiillinik caribou.

Some Ahiarmiut caribou spend the winter south of the treeline in Indian lands. Come spring, the caribou return to Inuit land, northwards through Contwoyto Lake and to the Kingauk area.

> They are big caribou, even the legs look so thick on the
> caribou from the south that are from the mainland.
> Because they eat moss, berry leaves, willows on the
> mainland during the winter. There probably is not too
> much for them to eat here on Kiillinik, but there is more
> grass and vegetation growing nowadays. They would
> return to the mainland where there is more vegetation
> for them to eat, a mixture of vegetation. There are all
> kinds of vegetation that grow down there. They would
> return to where there is more for them to eat.
>
> *Moses Koihok, 1999*

Some people have heard about and occasionally seen the very small caribou that are the size of yearlings although they are adults. Caribou from this herd live in the northern parts of Nunavut, north of Kiillinik. Known as Peary caribou, they are not discussed in this chronicle.

Qitirmiut from Hanigakhik, Ikaluktuuttiak, Kingauk, and Umingmaktuuk harvest the Kiillinik caribou during the fall, winter, and spring. People from Hanigakhik, Kingauk, and Umingmaktuuk hunt the Ahiarmiut caribou during the spring, summer, and fall seasons. In the summer and fall, when it is easy to travel from Kiillinik to the mainland, Qitirmiut from Ikaluktuuttiak also harvest the Ahiarmiut caribou, although there are lower numbers at these times of the year.

Since the 1970s, the ranges of the Ahiarmiut and Kiillinik caribou herds have been overlapping more than they did in the past, especially in the areas between Kingauk and Umingmaktuuk. The Ahiarmiut caribou have been moving farther north during the summer, and the Kiillinik caribou moving farther south during the winter.

During the spring, I have noticed some Barrenland
caribou up in Victoria Island and heading to Victoria
Island from the mainland. I guess maybe mixed breed.
I do not know.

George Kavanna, 1998

Since each herd's range has moved a little every year, caribou from different herds have interacted more than before. In the past ten to fifteen years, migration routes of the Ahiarmiut and Kiillinik caribou have come together more frequently, and individual caribou from the different herds have started to migrate jointly. Individuals or small groups will mingle during this time and create their own small herd before joining the larger herd.

One Qitirmiut theory about the creation of caribou herds is that new herds arise from the mixing of two other herds and that different herds have always overlapped and intermingled. Individuals from one herd might spend a year or two with another herd before coming back to their original herd.

THEORIES ABOUT
HERD ORIGINS

Do you know how the Kiillinik caribou came to be?
The Bathurst caribou met up with the Peary caribou.
Might not be, but that is what I think.

Naikak Hakongak, 2000

A few people think that a herd has emerged that is a mix of the Ahiarmiut and Kiillinik herds. The new herd, known to biologists as the Queen Maud herd, is known by some locals as the "Heinz 57" herd, because it is a mixture of the Kiillinik and Bathurst herds. Some Ahiarmiut caribou appear not to return south with the rest of the herd, which makes the herd seem larger. Instead, they stay around the Kingauk region. Some caribou from the Queen Maud herd stay around the Bathurst Inlet region all year.

Since most people do not distinguish between types of Ahiarmiut caribou, an Inuinnaqtun term for the "Queen Maud" herd has not yet gained popularity. Only one interviewee spoke about the differences between the herds, including the "Queen Maud" caribou.

Over in the mainland the caribou are much larger and darker than the ones from Victoria Island. Kiillinik caribou, the caribou are much smaller than the mainland caribou.... I have seen quite a bit of caribou in the Queen Maud Gulf, and the Kingauk caribou.... It is on the north side of upper Garry Lake where I have seen caribou. They are much bigger than the caribou from the upper mainland, say from the Queen Maud Gulf area. The caribou down here in Garry Lake are a lot bigger than the Queen Maud Gulf caribou and the Victoria Island caribou. I noticed they are a little bit bigger, way bigger than the Victoria Island caribou. I noticed they are much darker, darker and bigger. Those caribou I really like the *niqi* [meat], and I like the skin. They are really good for clothing, say for *qarliit, ilupaat, pualut,* or *qulittaat* [pants, inner parkas, mitts, or outer parkas]. I notice the caribou are much darker colour, south, upper from Garry Lakes than the Queen Maud Gulf caribou and the Victoria Island. I have seen both kinds, the Island caribou and the Barrenland caribou.

George Kavanna, 1998

MIXING OF CARIBOU HERDS

Mixing of Ahiarmiut and Kiillinik herds has become a common sight out on hunting trips. The overlap is related to the warmer weather experienced in the 1990s, which has meant caribou can find plants to eat on the tundra that are of better quality and support more individuals.

The caribou from the Bay Chimo and Bathurst Inlet area usually get together with those from the east and south. They would gather in one area. That is how the herd would grow.... The caribou would gather in the Bathurst Inlet area. They would get together with other herds from other areas. They would get together in that area during the spring. That is what they do.

Archie Komak, 1998

The caribou were mixed. They were mixed, few Island caribou, really small, and mainland caribou. Small, just a few. I guess they come all the way down. We noticed, my father in-law, right away, he said that he saw some Kiillinik caribou.

George Kavanna, 1999

The Ahiarmiut are probably more abundant [than the Kiillinik caribou].... They are not all the same. You can tell by the meat as well. There is a difference in the fur. I have never seen a Kiillinik caribou in the summer, only in the winter. They must be nice when their fur is thin in the summer.

Mabel Angulalik, 1998

During our first few years it was hard to get caribou because there were not so many. Now [the Bathurst herd] is coming from [the mainland], coming to Cambridge Bay.

Mackie Kaosoni, 1998

There are more caribou too. Even on Victoria Island there are lots. They are returning to Victoria Island. The bull caribou nowadays look like the winter caribou. They are starting to catch them.

Mary Kaniak, 1998

Factors That Affect Caribou Numbers

The size of caribou herds appears to be forever changing. Some years, there seem to be lots of caribou, whereas other years there are very few. Sometimes when there are fewer caribou, elders say it is simply because their instinct led them on a different route. In other words, it is not that there are really fewer caribou, only that they have decided to use migration routes that are farther away from those most familiar to locals.

It seems that the white people think that the numbers are declining, from what I have heard … at meetings, but sometimes wildlife goes a different route. And because of that, the numbers seem to be smaller.

Jessie Hagialok, 1998

Sometimes the caribou would go elsewhere. Even though there are lots, sometimes there would be no caribou around.

Archie Komak, 1998

In traditional times, knowing the actual number of caribou was not as critical to Qitirmiut as knowing whether the herd would migrate nearby or if there had been any large changes in the population level. Today, knowing the "true" number of caribou as well as the relative change in the population level is important in order to monitor environmental change and manage wildlife.

Caribou populations may fluctuate, but over time, populations remain generally constant. Reasons for changes in population include human activity (hunting, feeding dogs, mineral exploration), predation, climatic conditions, environmental factors, migration shifts, and the combination of these variables. These influences are discussed in detail in chapters 7 and 8. Human activity and climate are also presented briefly here.

HUMAN
ACTIVITY

[My husband] was saying, "Gee, I am catching caribou with babies in them. They will not have any baby caribou this summer." And his granny said, "Do not worry. You know there are lots. There are lots of other caribou. Probably lots of calves running around, by now." I guess she knows that there are probably hundreds and thousands of caribou around, and killing ten or fifteen with babies inside will not affect the population. But I know there is always a lot of other animals chasing after the little caribou and eating them also after they are born.

Anonymous C, 1998

People have asked that no mining take place near calving grounds because they are afraid it would diminish the number of caribou.

Paul Omilgoitok, 1998

CLIMATE

[In the spring] when the snow is soft and deep, some of the caribou would get skinny. They would get skinny when there is too much soft snow during the spring. When that is how it is. Some of the caribou would be okay.

Archie Komak, 1998

When the weather goes below freezing, some calves would freeze to death, and that would lessen the number of caribou.

Paul Omilgoitok, 1998

The snow was covered in ice and that is how the numbers [of caribou] dropped. The number of muskox went down too. The land was covered in sleet and there was no place for them to eat. This was by Wellington Bay.... I remember it well, but I cannot remember what year.... The snow was covered in ice. It had rained after a big snowfall. That is when some of the caribou had starved to death, but in another area of the land where it is not so rough, they were fine. Some areas were fine where it did not rain. There are not so many caribou around this area, but when it rained during the cold weather some caribou froze to death. I have seen that happen to a lot of caribou. There were muskox frozen as well. There were a lot of dead caribou on an island. A lot of dead bulls. A lot of them had died at once.... This was close to Ungahitak.

Archie Komak, 1998

In the past, when the caribou were travelling across from [Victoria] Island, when it is just freezing up between the island and the mainland, the ice broke and the caribou fell in. That was what Quighuk used to say.... Sometimes the ice would break up again after freeze-up.

George Kuptana, 1998

The question of whether caribou numbers are increasing or decreasing is not easy to answer. The response depends on people's perception of change as well as their references to particular time frames or seasons. Some people believe that the population is generally increasing. At the same time, many Qitirmiut report increases in certain types of caribou fatalities, most of which are directly linked to climatic influences.

In the 1990s, warmer temperatures earlier in the spring and during freeze-up led to more caribou drownings, deaths from heat exhaustion, and starvations. While skidooing, Qitirmiut noticed hundreds of caribou frozen along the shore, their antlers sticking out of the ice like a forest. Caribou can fall through the ice in the autumn when the temperatures are not cold enough to form ice thick enough for a safe crossing. In the spring, some caribou cross waterways through open cracks in the ice and cannot get out.

In the fall, warmer temperatures combined with sporadic freeze-thaw cycles and freezing rain can cause a layer of ice to form over the vegetation. This layer locks lichen into the ice and makes it impossible for caribou to dig through the snow to find nourishing tundra plants.

> [It was] raining heavily. That is what happened once in Bay Chimo, it must have been 1987. There was hardly any caribou to eat that time because of the ice on the snow. It was really slippery.
>
> *Charlie Keyok, 1998*

[The caribou] had starved to death because of sleet.
They had nowhere to eat. The ice was too thick....
They could not dig through it.

Moses Koihok, 1998

DECREASING
NUMBERS
Although some Qitirmiut report increasing numbers of caribou and others say populations are in decline, most people point out that assessing population change is not a simple equation. The interconnectedness and complexity in ecological relationships suggests that many factors are influencing populations to varying degrees.

We have seen large herds migrating, but nowadays
we do not see as many so I do not know. The bulls
would be together on their own path when everything goes well.

Mary Kaniak, 1998

Usually there are about two thousand caribou.... It is
slowing down ... these days. Maybe a change of climate
of going further to the east. Exploration? I do not
know. It is hard to say.

Allen Kapolak, 1998

There were no caribou at all in this area [Ikaluktuuttiak]....
People went to the mainland to hunt caribou during the
winter because there were none here ... in the 1970s.

Bessie Angulalik, 1998

There are a lot of Kiillinik caribou. During the winter,
the number seems lower because they winter inland.

Archie Komak, 1998

It seems that the numbers in the Ahiarmiut are declining. I do not know why. But here in Kingauk, there are

always a lot of caribou in the springtime. Lots in number. A couple of years ago there seemed to be lots in number as they were passing through.

Jessie Hagialok, 1998

This year there were hardly any [caribou]. This year, this spring, [there have been] hardly any caribou since April.... Less caribou compared to last year. Like the caribou never came from south.... There were always caribou around in the springtime [in other years]. Coming from south.

Doris Kingnektak, 1998

There are less [caribou] now. There are never as many as there used to be. They probably walk the other way.... There are less that come around. Even though they are high in numbers elsewhere.

Jessie Hagialok, 1998

Everything happens naturally. Fish and caribou existence is always shifting.

Paul Omilgoitok, 1998

Yeah. Everything in the environment happens naturally to wildlife. It is not the fault of the people.

Bessie Omilgoitok, 1998

It has changed. There are more animals now during the spring because the [Ahiarmiut] caribou would come across from the mainland like they used to a long time ago.

Mackie Kaosoni, 1998

A long time ago, it seemed like the [Kiillinik] caribou had vanished. There was no caribou at all. They were in abundance before they completely disappeared. For

MOSES KOIHOK,
IKALUKTUUTTIAK, 1998.

INCREASING
NUMBERS

how many years, I am not sure. They started catching the odd caribou. Now they are plentiful again. I remember when caribou started coming around again. Today, they even come close to town [Cambridge Bay].

Frank Analok, 1998

There probably are more [caribou] nowadays. There were not any caribou around Pond Inlet in the past, when I used to travel for meetings. Along those areas by Igloolik and the east, the islands and Iqaluit. Now the Kiillinik caribou are starting to show up in those areas. Sometimes they can be seen on airport runways in the eastern communities.

Moses Koihok, 1998

THE RETURN OF
KIILLINIK CARIBOU

Especially since the 1970s, the Kiillinik caribou have crossed to the mainland for the winter and moved as far south as Umingmaktuuk (see MAP 1). The herd appears to move farther south each year.

There was a time when there were no caribou at all. There were a lot of caribou, then later on there was less…. Sometimes they would catch a lot of caribou and sometimes less. When I became an adult, I think after we had children…. That was before the Kiillinik caribou started crossing. We came back here [to Umingmaktuuk] in the 1970s. They returned like they used to in the past. They are always around now. It is that way now except the white caribou are coming too, the smaller ones. The mainland caribou are darker and bigger. They come down like they used to in the past…. This was how it was told. There was absolutely no caribou on [Victoria] Island. I know they have returned like they did in the past.

George Kuptana, 1998

I remember a long time ago when there were less caribou and muskox. When the caribou numbers were going up in the past, about the same time the white men started coming around.

Archie Komak, 1998

[Caribou have known to cross ice] for as long as they have been around. Before we were even born, they have always travelled to the mainland then back. They would head back to Victoria Island in April and May. They would stay on the island during the spring thaw.... The Kiillinik caribou would go to Bay Chimo, going through Ikalulialuk [Island]. The Ahiarmiut and Kiillinik caribou would sometimes get together.... Caribou would come from different areas and gather. They would go down to the shoreline from the west. Caribou would come and go from all directions, to Igloolik and other settlements like Hall Beach, Rankin Inlet. Caribou would migrate in the winter. They would winter there. They would go and winter in the east, part of the mainland. They do not always stay in one area. They would come from all directions and mix sometimes.

Moses Koihok, 1998

95

A long time ago, people would travel to [Victoria] Island [from the mainland] when there was no caribou. The caribou would not come across. Must be close to a hundred, the number of caribou started coming around. I am getting old now and the caribou are showing again. My father-in-law used to tell me that there used to be a lot of caribou on the island and they would hunt with a bow and arrow. They did not have rifles then, when I was born, when I was just a child.

George Kuptana, 1998

In the past there were hardly any caribou. The caribou started coming around since we have been in Umingmaktuuk. There are usually caribou at Tahikaffaaluk, on the other side of Bay Chimo....
There were less probably in 1978. There were a lot of seals though.

Charlie Keyok, 1998

GEORGE KAPOLAK HANILIAK GOES HUNTING WITH HIS SON KEVIN, KINGAUK, 1998.

For generations, Qitirmiut have observed caribou herds mixing, their ranges overlapping, and their migration routes changing. As a result of these shifts, people changed their camp locations or suffered the consequences of having little or no caribou. Caribou ranges shift with habitat, predators, or climate, and due to other environmental factors. As ranges overlap and caribou from different herds mingle, "new" herds emerge, with the combined characteristics of both herds. In the Bathurst Inlet region, both the Ahiarmiut and Kiillinik caribou herds, plus any sub-herds that may be emerging from these two, continue to be essential to Qitirmiut. As the herds change, so do Qitirmiut hunting, cultural, and ceremonial practices. This has been, and always will be, the way of the caribou.

7 Distribution and Movement of Caribou

Caribou are always on the move: their need to migrate is as basic as their need to eat, drink, and mate. Their migration routes are always shifting, partly because they eat up most of the tundra along their traditional routes. Caribou also trample and graze tundra in calving areas, so they soon have to find other regions for migration and calving. Bugs, wind, heat, and the weather also affect where caribou migrate.

Qitirmiut understanding of caribou distribution and movements, illustrated in MAP 4 (see PAGE 178), comes from observing caribou throughout the seasons and over several years. When elders and hunters are on the land, they are always watching for caribou and reporting their sightings. In this way, word of where the caribou can be found spreads quickly and informs hunters.

see PAGE 178

Caribou are found "everywhere," "anywhere," and "all over" the tundra. Caribou are not fussy about where they are, although on a small scale caribou prefer certain areas, for example, where the tundra vegetation is especially healthy or green. On a large scale, caribou are found throughout the land and in many kinds of landscapes. There are predictable movements of caribou as they migrate northwards in the spring and southwards in the fall.

CARIBOU ARE EVERYWHERE

> They do not always go in one direction; they are all over the land around here and here. The land is full of caribou. They would walk in all directions.
>
> *May Algona, 1999*

> I do not know exactly what route they would take going north. When it is hot out, they would walk in any direction. They would go over the rough areas too, heading north. Going south it was like they travelled without straying…. It seemed like they would do anything heading north. It was hot outside, that is why.
>
> *Nellie Hikok, 1999*

> Even when they are walking slowly, they would reach their destination. I have seen them. Like they have always done, they walk wherever they want to walk…. They would walk all over the land. There is no need to write it down.
>
> *John Akana, 1998*

> The caribou would travel in one direction, going south, towards the centre of the mainland. They would head south in the fall. When the weather gets warmer in the

spring, they would head up from the south. They would come towards the ocean. That is the way the caribou travel.... Their ways are not all the same.

Archie Komak, 1998

Around the middle of June, we saw a big herd of caribou around Bay Chimo. The whole area was just white and you could see them for miles, Bathurst [Ahiarmiut] caribou. That was seven years ago. You could see caribou along the river walking all day. You could see, even after twelve hours, the caribou still moving. [It was] just like a waterfall going down a hill. You could see white all day. You could walk in between them and they would still be walking. There were wolves among them too.

George Panegyuk, 1997

Year after year, millions of caribou hooves have trampled the tundra and gravel ridges and carved deep trails along their migration routes. After the caribou have migrated, their presence continues to be felt along these trails, in the bits of fur that have settled on the land and rivers, or the caribou bones remaining from wolf kills. Broken branches that have been trampled or half eaten and the piles of caribou pellets tossed about like spent bullets are also evidence of migrating caribou.

THE LAND GETS WORN

Even before the days that we were born, the caribou would take those same routes. That is how the land gets worn. The trails would get wide. They would make trails along the rivers, by the mouths of the rivers, and

FRANK ANALOK, IKALUKTUUTTIAK, 1998.

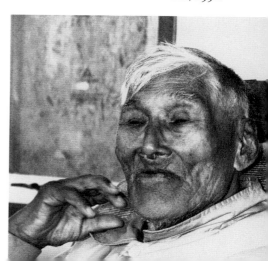

the trails would get wide and deep over the years.... The caribou would take the same routes because they have always travelled those routes.... The trails look like they have been drawn in when you are flying over the lakes. There are a lot of trails that look like they have been drawn.

Moses Koihok, 1998

You can tell where they have tread when there are so many of them.

Mabel Angulalik, 1998

When the caribou are migrating, they would go in one direction. Going down that way or coming up, they travel any route. That is what the animals do.... Their routes are not hard to spot. Whatever route they have taken the year before they use again. That is what they usually do. They usually go where they can find food.

Archie Komak 1998

The Annual Migration Cycle

The caribou migration cycle begins with *atiqtat*, the spring migration northwards to the *auyiviit*, summer grounds or ocean, and continues with *kilumuuqtut*, the fall migration southwards and inland to *ukiiviit*, the winter grounds. A caribou calf is able to walk and join the other caribou within an hour of being born. Mother and calf move short distances around the calving area, eating and getting strong before the southward migration begins. In August, small herds of caribou consisting of cows and calves, yearlings, and a bull or two begin the trek. The majority of the bulls follow within the next few weeks.

After the rut is over in late October, Ahiarmiut caribou congregate into larger herds and continue the migration towards the treeline for the winter months. In the early spring, after several months of foraging in the trees, the cows lead the herd northwards towards the calving grounds, where the annual cycle begins again. In contrast, the Kiillinik caribou have their calving grounds in the northern regions of Victoria Island and migrate to the mainland for the winter months. The following knowledge about the migration cycle of the caribou is divided by herd types: Ahiarmiut and Kiillinik.

When the caribou are heading north in the spring, the *kan'ngalaq*, there is no beginning and no end. Even though they are quite a ways [away,] they would get close sometimes.

Nellie Hikok, 1999

Sometimes they would calve during their migration.

Moses Koihok, 1998

The cows with or without calves come [from inland] first. The bulls come from the east in the spring following the cows.... The bulls and cows would head north in the summer, then head south together.... When they are calving, they head north.

John Akana, 1998

Usually the cows come first and the bulls come later.... Nowadays, there are more cows than what I have seen. Maybe the bulls take a different route. Take a detour.

Allen Kapolak, 1998

Here at Pellatt Lake, I see lots of caribou going through during the spring and fall. Just passing through. Maybe a couple of days, not very long though. Sometimes there are millions. When you go to sleep there are millions behind the cabin and next day, when you wake up, there is nothing. It depends on what they want to eat.

Anonymous C, 1998

NOAH KUPTANA, UMINGMAKTUUK, 1998.

[When they are migrating through Kingauk/Bathurst Inlet], caribou take a month to pass, maybe, or something like that. May and June.

Martha Akoluk, 1998

Every spring, what they call *utiqtun*, they would come down to the ocean. They probably came from the wooded areas from far.

Nellie Hikok, 1999

Spring Migration of Kiillinik Caribou

During the spring, [caribou] would cross [from Arctic Sound and Rideout Island towards Elu Inlet, then across to Cambridge Bay], heading up to Victoria Island... .The migration routes, they have not changed. Before spring they would head up here, passing through Elu Inlet.

Archie Komak, 1998

[The Kiillinik caribou] leave the Brown Sound area in April. There are hardly any more caribou. They go back north. They come, stay there all winter, and head north again. Ahiarmiut caribou, they come here too.

Doris Kingnektak, 1998

Last spring we saw quite a few in April. In April 1997 we were camping and we saw lots of caribou migrating…. Anywhere from on the mainland…. They sort of make a beeline straight northwards…. I think in the early 1980s we used to have to go about thirty miles west of Ikaluktuuttiak to get caribou in the fall and in the spring, and then as the 1980s started to close off, the caribou seemed to come closer towards town…. When you think about it, they go along at a certain length of an area on the way up and the next year they will move over a little bit.

Naikak Hakongak, 1998

The cows can be seen in April or May, coming across from the mainland…. During the month of May, the Kiillinik caribou usually head to the calving grounds.

Frank Analok, 1998

When the antlers have grown on the bulls, they would gather in one place…. Near the end of October, around mid-October, they would get together. The bulls and cows would head south together. They would go right to the lakes, the bulls and cows, heading south.

Archie Komak, 1998

The yearlings and the young ones get fat so they could go further down inland. They feed when the rest of them are mating, the young ones and the yearlings.

Annie Komak, 1998

Before August, after they have calved, they walk inland this way [inland to the south]…. Some of them go this way [southeast or southwest] and others go inland.

John Akana, 1998

FALL MIGRATION
OF AHIARMIUT
CARIBOU

In the fall time they head inland. When it starts to get cold, during freeze-up, the Kiillinik caribou will travel inland. During the spring thaw, they would come across from the mainland to calve and spend the summer close by the ocean.... When the caribou are migrating and get close to lkaluktuuttiak, in the fall.... From here near Kangigyuk [Prince Albert Sound] down from the west side going east, heading inland in the fall. They would travel by Ikaluktuuttiak.

Frank Analok, 1998

In the fall they head inland. They would roam on the land during the winter. When the ocean is frozen they would cross from the mainland going back and forth.... Yes, the caribou never stay in one area. They roam around. They are never in one area for long periods. They would travel their route. Sometimes it seems like there are no caribou at all, because they are constantly moving.

Mabel Angulalik, 1998

This whole place [around Hanigakhik] had caribou all winter.... There is hardly any more caribou. They go back north. They come [to Hanigakhik], stay there all winter, and head north again. Kiillinik caribou, they come here.... Heading north probably in April. Coming November 15th. I never go caribou hunting east of Umingmaktuuk. Only see caribou there, coming and going.

Doris Kingnektak, 1998

Reasons for Change in Caribou Movements and Migrations

Many factors influence the migration patterns of caribou. Caribou have a natural instinct to migrate that is triggered by seasonal clues, such as the length or heat of the day or the thickness of the sea ice. Caribou must adapt their migrations to many changes in the climate and the terrain.

[Migrations] change a lot, because they used to come right through here. West and more east now. They used to come right through Kingauk.

Martha Akoluk, 1998

He said that there used to be thousands and thousands of caribou at Elliot Point. Maybe for the whole day, just passing through. But this time, he said there are none.... Not thousands. Behind the cabin on Elliot Point, he said that this year they are not coming through there. They were not really coming through there last year also. I guess they change their route, which depends on which way they want to go. We cannot tell them where to go!

Anonymous C, 1998

During the winter, sometimes caribou would not come this far up so we would stay at Hanningayuk. Sometimes they would catch a lot of caribou for the winter when there was plenty to catch during freeze-up. When the caribou were inland during the winter, there would be none around. That is how it used to be in the past.... I remember during the winter there would never be any caribou at all. Now they are always around.

Mary Kaniak, 1998

REASONS FOR CHANGES IN CARIBOU MIGRATION ROUTES AND TIMING INCLUDE THE WEATHER, WIND, ICE AND SNOW CONDITIONS, THE TIME OF YEAR, INSECTS, AND HUMAN ACTIVITY.

Whether or not Qitirmiut said caribou change their migration routes partly depended on their definition of "change." Some elders said that the migration routes have always been the same. Their concept of change may be from a more long-term or large-scale perspective.

INTERPRETATIONS OF CHANGE IN MIGRATION ROUTES

The travel routes have not changed. It has been mentioned in the past that they would take one route coming from the south. They would head inland in the fall. They would walk south. They gather together inland.

Annie Kaosoni, 1999

In contrast, other Qitirmiut said that the migration routes are always changing. Perhaps they look at the world from a more close-up perspective, as if through a magnifying glass. As a result, their perception of change is very different from that of somebody who views the world as if looking down from outer space. Changing migration routes must be considered in the context of questions of scale and people's perceptions.

ICE AND SNOW
CONDITIONS

They used to always come this way [through Kingauk].… I think it might be the soft snow. If there is too much soft snow, they go the other way, where there is less snow. Sometimes they have to go the other way. When the ice is breaking up too, they have to go a different route.

Martha Akoluk, 1998

Sometimes they would use the trails in the soft snow. Some would avoid the snow and walk on the ground.

Paul Omilgoitok, 1998

One year we had freezing rain around Bathurst and they changed their migration because of freezing rain. In the spring, it gets really slippery and dangerous.

George Kapolak Haniliak, 1998

WIND AND
INSECTS

The wind direction changes caribou movement on hot days. Too many mosquitoes! They would face the wind direction to keep cold and keep the mosquitoes away. [Otherwise, it is] too hot!

Lena Kamoayok, 1998

They would go towards the wind when there are too many mosquitoes.… During the hot summer months, June and July, wherever the wind is coming from they would go towards that direction. That is what they normally do, even in the winter.

Moses Koihok, 1998

I am worried that if there is too much mining going on up here in the North, caribou might just change their route and not come around completely. Not come around their normal migration routes, and people are going to have to move further and further for caribou. It is going to be harder for everyone up north to go hunting.

Anonymous C, 1998

If they could not allow mining companies to explore and use explosives on calving grounds. The caribou get afraid.

Archie Komak, 1998

Those mining companies … do not bother the caribou, so I do not mind them.… When the caribou are not being bothered, they do not run away. The caribou usually stand outside the building of the mines.

May Algona, 1999

I think caribou calving grounds, during caribou migrations, when there is exploration going on around here, might be good to leave the area alone. Leave there or until they get through or have their calves. [A good distance before the mines would have to shut down] would be thirteen to sixteen kilometres. If there is not too much noise, I think it would not bother them too much.

Allen Kapolak, 1998

The [mining companies] should shut down when the caribou are coming through. About sixteen kilometres [from the caribou]. They have got pretty good ears and eyes. You know it really bothers the caribou.…They get more sensitive when they are calving.

George Kapolak Haniliak, 1998

This land [near Bathurst Inlet] should not be mined at all. This is where the caribou always walk. If there were anything placed here, there would be nothing for the caribou to eat. That would not be too good, because caribou are all the people eat. There should be no mining at all here at the calving grounds.… The land should not be broken anywhere.… It is our land and our traditional camping grounds. There should be no mining there.… The land should not be spoiled at all.

May Algona, 1999

SHIPPING

The ships can run during the summer months (June, July, August, and September). If they can stop production in September, October, and November.… Shipping should be stopped in October and November in order for the caribou to migrate.… What we would like to see is the ships put to a stop during the caribou migration south in October and November. That is the time the caribou cross to the mainland.… Since there will be a lot of work going on and the caribou usually head back to Victoria Island in April and May, production should be stopped for those two months as well.

Moses Koihok, 1998

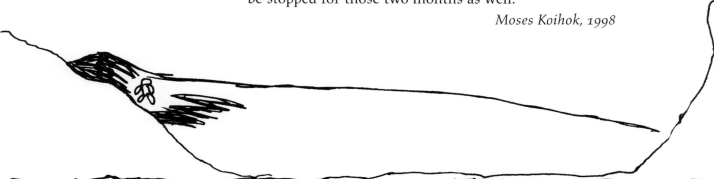

[The caribou] probably get tired of hearing helicopters like I do.

George Kuptana, 1997

I think they fly too low and the caribou start running. [I have] seen a lot of that. When choppers start flying around, they fly too low and get the caribou running.

Allen Kapolak, 1998

[Caribou] would run away when they hear helicopters. That is how they are right now.… Some caribou do not mind the mining going on and helicopters flying around in the summer and spring.… [The caribou] run away; sometimes they just stand there.

Charlie Keyok, 1998

I do not think it would be okay to put a road near Kingauk. It is okay to put a road where they say it would be all right, but not in this area. If there is too much traffic, there would be fewer caribou.... There are always a lot of caribou and it will not be a problem for the vehicles, but it will be hard when there are fewer caribou.... There would be fewer caribou around here if there is too much traffic.... [If there was a road], they should stop [traffic] in June and August.

Paul Omilgoitok, 1998

QUALITY OF TUNDRA
VEGETATION

Nowadays there are not many caribou going there [east side of Bathurst Inlet]. They go here [west side of Bathurst Inlet] instead. There must be a shortage of food for them there.

Meyok Omilgoitok, 1998

The caribou from Kiillinik are heading to the mainland where food is more abundant. Victoria Island has no willows and there is hardly any wood.... There is no moss and lichen here on Victoria Island.... That is where the caribou would go to spend the winter, where there is more for them to eat.

Moses Koihok, 1998

When they come through my place [Pellatt Lake] ... all the vegetation and everything is really green. Nothing touched the vegetation. Green, totally green, the whole tundra is green. And when the caribou come through, and they finish with it, it is all totally brown, everything is all eaten up and just stomped to the ground. And when they come through, once they pass in the year, the caribou, the smell would be there for weeks, the whole land is stenched with urine.

Bobby Algona, 1999

Traditionally, Qitirmiut watched caribou and paid close attention to their behaviour. Caribou tend to move at varying speeds, at certain times of the day, and in a particular order.

ACTIVITY

In the summer, in the evening, when it starts getting dark, they would walk along the shore and graze. They would walk on lakeshores and graze.… During the day, they would graze and crouch on the ground. During the night, they would lie on the ground.

Frank Analok, 1998

PACE OF MOVEMENT

When the caribou start moving together, we can hear them when they are running. We could hear them running just like horses.… Just like thunder. When they are running, lots of noise, and you could hear their antlers banging together.

Annie Komak, 1998

They seem to be moving faster in the spring than in the fall. In the summer there was some too, always some running around.

Anonymous C, 1998

When the snow is melting, they would tire out easily when they are walking on soft snow. That is what we have seen. During the winter though, when it [the snow] is hard enough to walk on, they get around faster.

Annie Kaosoni, 1998

JAMES PANIOYAK, IKALUKTUUTTIAK, 1997.

When it gets warmer, they probably speed up to get to their calving grounds. When it is cool, they just take their time, but if it gets warmer, they have to speed up so that they can get to their calving grounds. They must have internal clocks, maybe that is just what ticks. The alarm starts to go! If it is too cold, then they

try to stay put in an area until it warms up, and then they can keep going. You never really see any caribou moving when it is stormy. They are always lying down conserving their energy. Whenever I used to go out, that has been my observation in the years that I have been travelling: when the weather is stormy, they find an area where they can lie down easily for their food. And they stay around there until the weather gets a little bit better for travelling, and then they keep moving unless you disturb them.

Naikak Hakongak, 1998

WATER CROSSINGS

When they are migrating, it is a great big rush to be on the move. Really rushing, they are really going, running, running constantly all the time…. Really rocky, rough, and … little calves get their feet caught on the rocks and they never get up again. They stumble and they never get up again. They just get stomped on almost to a powder. Whole bones, bones and everything, churned right up from all the feet, nothing left of the baby calf. In the river crossing, they are crossing, there is just no room to move. There is a great big herd swimming across and some of those little baby calves they accidentally get caught under the herd and they never get out again until the

MACKIE KAOSONI,
IKALUKTUUTTIAK, 1998.

herd pass through. And they come floating up in the water after the herd comes. Found five of them one year like that. Five baby calves. Once they get the urge to move, they do not stop until they have to or get to the place where they are going.... When [caribou] are crossing rivers, springtime, they are sort of taking it easy going north. It is not as dangerous for them to go across the lake. They just take their time. River crossings, they just take their time, no rush to get across, no danger to other members of the herd. But once they turn around in July, they want to head south. I do not know why that is, they just want to go all at once, get it over and done with, and just going constantly, running mostly.... It is a big rush to get across lakes. Once one gets across, everybody else wants to keep up, so as soon as they get off that water [they] just want to catch up to the rest of the herd. They usually run out of the water and run.

Bobby Algona, 1999

When the caribou are going to the other side of the lakes or rivers, they would get across at a water crossing pretty quick.

Archie Komak, 1998

Caribou, just head and antlers and a back, head and antlers and a back, swimming across a lake. They can swim a maximum of two miles. Five miles would be a bit of a stretch.

Naikak Hakongak, 1998

HERD LEADERSHIP

One summer when the caribou were migrating south again, caribou were moving too fast for us to start to shoot ... so we just shot the leader, the lead cow. Every other caribou just started standing around, did not know where to go. That is when we started choosing caribou we wanted. Still moving too fast, we have seen one and did not know which one to shoot, and so we just shot the lead cow and all the rest just scattered.

Bobby Algona, 1999

They always have a female leader, a cow without calf. They change every year.... The caribou take turns leading when they are walking.

Mary Kaniak, 1998

The cows would lead when they are heading inland in the fall. During the fall, I have seen that when it starts to cool off.

Mackie Kaosoni, 1999

JIMMY MANIYOGINA, IKALUKTUUTTIAK, 1998.

116

For as long as Qitirmiut can remember, caribou have always migrated to and moved about the Bathurst Inlet region. Elders and hunters depended on their knowledge of caribou distribution and migrations in order to survive. Such knowledge was sometimes difficult to obtain, because caribou behaviour cannot always be predicted.

From a large scale-perspective, caribou have traditional migration routes that do not change. From a small-scale perspective, movements and migrations shift according to a combination of factors such as weather, climate, insects, and human activity. As in the past, Qitirmiut continue to observe carefully any changes in caribou movements and migrations that inform their understanding of caribou.

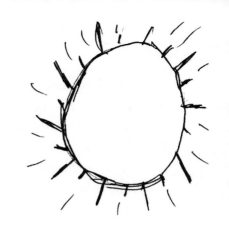

8 Caribou Predators

There has always been a natural balance between caribou and other animals. One year there may be more caribou and another year there may be fewer. The weather and how it influences the land and wildlife is most important in this balance, yet the impact of predators on caribou is also key.

Next to people, wolves kill the most caribou. Once a caribou is killed, grizzlies, foxes, hares, wolverines, and birds feed on the remains.

Caribou get eaten fast. No matter what, caribou gets eaten alive. A whole pack of wolves can finish one big caribou in half the night. I have come across caribou carcasses that have just been recently eaten. You can usually tell when it has been eaten or when it has been caught or how long it was there by fresh blood. On the ground, no blood on the ground, few days old. Wolf is usually the one [to kill caribou], but I witnessed a bear tackle caribou. I witnessed wolf tackle caribou, I witnessed wolverine tackle caribou, even a fox try to tackle a caribou. Everything likes caribou meat. It is pretty much similar, the way they hunt caribou. Stalk and kill.

Bobby Algona, 1999

I see some cows they try to protect their caribou, like charging at wolves or people, but mostly the wolves, I think, and foxes. I have seen caribou charging at other animals trying to keep their young ones safe from other animals.

George Kavanna, 1998

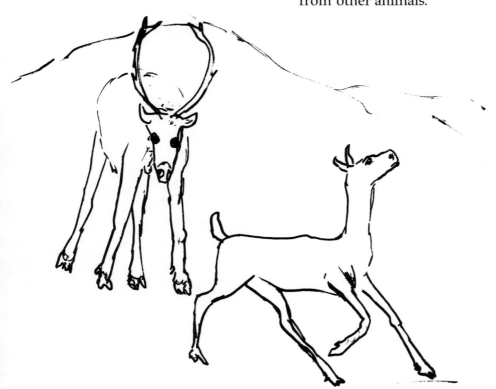

Qitirmiut are important caribou predators. Although most Qitirmiut do not have to hunt for subsistence, they take what they need for their immediate and extended family. For some hunters, this can be as many as to five caribou per year. For others, the number can be closer to seventy.

> I try to get lots of caribou during the fall time so my
> family, relatives, and the elders could have caribou
> through the cold winter. In the springtime, I get
> enough caribou to make dry meat. I would say about
> between thirty to fifty caribou per year, to last through
> the winter and the cold months of the winter.
>
> *George Kavanna, 1998*

Amaqqut (wolves) are smart and skilled hunters of healthy caribou as well as the sick, injured, weak, and young caribou, especially near the calving grounds in May. Amaqqut have an important impact on caribou population levels. When there are no caribou, there will be no wolves, and when there are lots of caribou, there will be lots of wolves.

Amaqqut are capable predators because they are fast runners, with the females being the quickest pursuers. As a pack, amaqqut are experts at chasing and killing caribou. Perhaps because they are such good hunters, amaqqut are more numerous than other predators and hence have a competitive advantage. Amaqqut depend heavily on caribou. When there are no caribou, wolf pups often die.

> The wolves must get more [caribou] because they are
> fast. There must be more of them. I have heard that
> the female wolves would lead a pack.... That is what
> we have seen. We have heard of it as well. The females
> are faster. They would attack the [caribou from] behind.
>
> *Mackie Kaosoni, 1998*

> Yes, because [the females] are lighter.
>
> *Annie Kaosoni, 1998*

BUSTER KAILIK,
KUGLUKTUK, 1999.

CARIBOU TRY TO PROTECT
THEMSELVES FROM DANGER
IN SEVERAL WAYS. BUT
DESPITE THEIR BEST
EFFORTS, CARIBOU DO
NOT USUALLY ESCAPE A
HUNGRY PREDATOR.
WOLVES ARE THE MOST
SKILLED PREDATORS
APART FROM HUMANS.

For wolf, it is the female that does the catching. Very fast, that female wolf. They run up to sixty and seventy kilometres an hour. And the female wolf is the one that drags the caribou down, bites it on the tail, the feet, anywhere, just slow him down. From behind, the male wolf finally catches up and grabs it by the throat. The female would let go and take a rest.

Bobby Algona, 1999

The wolves … kill more [caribou]. I have seen a wolf chase a caribou, but not kill it. As soon as the caribou sees a wolf, it goes straight for the water when they are trying to get away from the wolves. [I have] seen a wolf chasing one.… As soon as the caribou hits the water, the wolf will not chase them. The wolf stops.

George Kapolak Haniliak, 1998

The wolves are always eating caribou. They eat calves and bulls too.… Wolves catch more caribou because there are more wolves on the land. There are more [wolves] than wolverines and grizzlies. Because there are more [wolves], they catch more caribou.… My son and I have seen wolves chasing caribou when we are snowmobiling. Sometimes it is hard to catch caribou.… I have seen wolves attacking and killing a caribou. We have seen that quite a bit in Umingmaktuuk.… We have seen wolves catching caribou at Hanningayuk.… There are a lot of wolves.

Charlie Keyok, 1998

This is where the caribou would cross over water … this area is full of wolf dens.… [The wolves] know where the crossings are.

Buster Kailik, 1999

In the late 1980s, I remember the wolves were eating lots of bulls. All over the place: Umingmaktuuk, mainland. I remember travelling and seeing them not too far from the trail—wolf kills. Even talking to hunters, they would say they would see dead bulls. More dead bulls, because they were easier to catch because they are tired after the rut. They lose a lot of weight and strength.

Naikak Hakongak, 2000

My brother-in-law and I went for a day trip down to towards the Elu Inlet to go wolf hunting. We caught up to some wolf tracks and we followed them in a very large circle probably about fifty-two miles. The wolf was following a small herd of caribou. On the way, we see that the wolf wove in and out of the caribou herd, chased them towards the west. Then the caribou turned north, and then they turned east. They kept running. You could see the caribou or wolf tracks go in and out and then turn back south, and it led us back to where we were. After about an hour, we saw these little drops of blood along the trail. And then the drops of blood got bigger, and then the drops of blood had caribou fur in them, and then you could see the caribou fur. And we crested this hill and there was this caribou with its haunches all torn up. Around its throat was torn up too. And we caught up to that wolf maybe about ten minutes later. It had been the one that attacked that caribou. It followed that caribou herd, just kept following until it found one and it said, "I could take this one down no problem," so it just kept following. May 1995: Started at Caribou Lake, and made a fifty-two–mile circle. Just west, north, east, south, and back to where

QITIRMIUT HAVE LEARNED ABOUT HUNTING CARIBOU BY WATCHING THE WAYS THAT WOLVES CHASE AND KILL CARIBOU.

NAIKAK HAKONGAK, IKALUKTUUTTIAK, 2000.

it basically began at the chase. That is the closest I
have ever come to seeing wolves actually catching or
killing caribou. Probably died just soon after we left it,
'cause we looked at it and it was barely even able to stand
up and breathe. So we just left it alone and went looking
for the caribou or looking for the wolf.

Naikak Hakongak, 1998

GRIZZLY BEARS
When hunting caribou, it is not only important to think like a caribou, but
also to sense like a successful predator. For example, in the days of hunting with
markers and blinds, it was important for Qitirmiut to hunt as a group, much
like wolves hunt as a pack. (See chapter 3 for a description of Inuit hunting
strategies and techniques.)

Aghat (grizzly bears) are rarely fast enough to be superior caribou predators.
Aghat mainly eat berries, fresh shoots, roots, and small mammals, but they also
hunt caribou.

I have seen a grizzly chasing a calf once. I caught sight
of it as they were disappearing behind a hill. The grizzly
probably ate it. This was when we spent the summer
here [west of Bathurst Lake, near Aniaghiugvik].

Paul Omilgoitok, 1998

Grizzlies can quickly catch caribou. They would wait
along the seashore.

Lena Kamoayok, 1998

> There was nothing but caribou and [my friend] said that they saw grizzly bears with their cubs.... There were thousands of caribou.... There were wolves following grizzly bears with cubs.... They just followed [the caribou] along eskers.
>
> *Naikak Hakongak, 1998*

Although only a few Qitirmiut have actually seen aghat actively killing a caribou, many stories of aghat have been passed down. Hungry aghat, especially in the spring, can be dangerous and should be avoided.

Qalviit (wolverines) tend to be scavengers of caribou meat. Qalviit steal **WOLVERINES** foxes from people's traps, drag caribou meat away from campsites, and dig out caribou meat from rock caches during the fall and winter. In the past, when Qitirmiut relied on this cached meat, such a disturbance could be devastating.

> Even [though] the wolverine is small, it can still get a caribou.
>
> *Charlie Keyok, 1998*

> Wolverines eat caribou as well.
>
> *Annie Kaosoni, 1998*

Tiriganniat (Arctic fox), *kajuqtuq* (red fox), and *kiahirutilik* (cross fox) eat **FOXES** lemmings, baby birds, and a variety of eggs found on the tundra, as well as caribou meat from a predator's kill. Tiriganniat are known to co-operate with bears, helping them find injured or sick caribou. They do this by yelping when there is caribou activity, especially if the caribou is injured, sick, or old.

> I would not know if foxes catch caribou. They do get calves though. They prey on calves because they are small.
>
> *Charlie Keyok, 1998*

> Foxes eat [caribou] as well.
>
> *Annie Kaosoni, 1998*

BIRDS   Seagulls, ravens, ruddy turnstones, and hawks often feed themselves and their young on caribou remains, especially on the sea ice. From a far distance, one can sometimes see birds flying in circles above a kill site. Ravens usually caw and point with their wings to an area where there is caribou commotion to make it easier for predators to find. Small birds such as snow buntings and longspurs scavenge maggots off caribou remains.

> All the seagulls always go for [the caribou guts]. The seagulls and the foxes, and so nothing is wasted from a caribou.
>
> *Anonymous C, 1998*

SMALL ANIMALS   Caribou antlers found everywhere on the land always have teeth marks from *hikhiit* and *avin'ngat* (ground squirrels and lemmings) and other animals, including wolves, wolverines, and foxes. Antlers are important for making the bones of these small animals strong.

     Many predators and scavengers benefit from caribou that migrate into the Kitikmeot region. Wolves kill the most caribou, especially calves on or nearby calving grounds. People and grizzlies are also important predators. Wildlife that hunt caribou keep the herds in balance by preying on the sick, weak, or injured animals. Such predation is all part of a food chain that supports many other animals. By natural means, the delicate Arctic ecosystem is maintained.

9 Habitat and Forage of Caribou

Caribou are clever enough to identify places where there is healthy food and where they can escape from the elements, insects, predators, and difficult terrain. These places for feeding and refuge include islands, shorelines, snow patches, valleys, and spots that are either damp or shaded.

Habitat Preferred by Caribou

Caribou often gather along the shores of lakes, rivers, and the ocean. Caribou are like people in that they seek out shorelines where high winds keep the insects away and the temperatures cooler. In addition, shorelines provide easy escape from predators and the heat when caribou can find relief in the water. Moist areas also support vegetation that is large and lush and good for both forage and shade.

Caribou often keep cool by lying on patches of snow in the spring. Snow that is deep or covered by a hard layer of ice is difficult to paw through for food, so caribou try to avoid these areas. They also look for migration routes away from difficult terrain. For example, caribou walk around rather than over mountains if they are too steep or rocky.

COOL, MOIST SHORELINES, AWAY FROM INSECTS AND PREDATORS

In the summertime, in the evening, when it gets dark, they would walk along the shore and graze. Caribou like to eat on the lakeshores where the grass is plenty. When it is hot outside, the caribou would go on the shores of the ocean, where it is cooler.... Caribou stay in the shaded areas.... In the shade as well as by the lakes. By the lakeshores, as well as shaded areas wherever they can find what they like to eat.

Mabel Angulalik, 1998

When the weather is warm, the caribou would stay in shaded areas during the summer. People would look for caribou in the shade during warm days. It is easier for the hunters to get close to them.

Frank Analok, 1998

When it starts to get dark, they go to the lakes.... During the nighttime caribou stay by lakeshores, which makes it easier for them to escape from wolves.

Mackie Kaosoni, 1998

The caribou stay alongshore in the summer in June and July.... To stay away from the bugs and to keep cool, [caribou] stay by the ocean and the islands.

Moses Koihok, 1998

In really marshy areas, or the bottom of the hills in the summertime, lots of vegetation on the bottom of those hills, [caribou] tend to stay in there. In the hollows, summertime, where it is cooler.... Maybe less insects.... Just for the coolness of being below, I guess, in the summertime.

Bobby Algona, 1999

[Caribou go] along the shore of lakes and the ocean.... [and] close to water, where there is moisture. They would eat more where there is moisture in the summer. They would look for what they like to eat. They know what they like to eat.

Charlie Keyok, 1998

They probably eat all sorts of vegetation. Whatever is sprouting on the land. They are constantly on the move and would often stop to eat as they are travelling … on lakeshores, whatever is sprouting. Moist vegetation like grass. Whatever is sprouting on the shores of lakes, riversides. Wherever there is moisture.... The caribou usually go to the ocean along the coast. They can also be seen swimming in the lakes, staying away from mosquitoes.

Frank Analok, 1998

They are always along the coastline. When there are too many mosquitoes, they would gather and go in circles to get rid of mosquitoes.

Moses Koihok, 1998

Another reason why caribou spend time along the shores of the sea is so they can lick the salt from the rocks. It may be that caribou like the taste and need the sea salt to keep healthy. Caribou sometimes eat seaweed.

Favourite Caribou Forage

Urjuk
Moss

Uqauyaq
Lichen

Iviit
Grasses and Sedges

Avaalaqiaq
Birch and Alders

Uqpik
Willow

Kaiptauyat
Mushrooms

They would lie on the patches of remaining snow to keep cool.

Mabel Angulalik, 1998

The caribou and other animals like it best when the snow is not covered in sleet.… When the snow gets too hard, when it is really cold, they would stay where there is less snow. When there is too much water in the spring as well, when it rains too much, the number of squirrels would go down. That is how it is. When the land is covered in ice, the caribou would get skinny.

Charlie Keyok, 1998

When the land is not covered in sleet, the caribou would graze, uncovering patches of snow and eating as they go along.

Frank Analok, 1998

Easy Routes

They like to follow eskers … they just go along eskers and they will go along eskers for so long on top of eskers. It is just like a road … and it is really nice on top 'cause you get a breeze.… In the winter, they are mostly inland where they can get to the vegetation easily. And plus [this] area is a little bit rocky too, so they go somewhere else instead.

Naikak Hakongak, 1998

Sometimes there are caribou that pass there on big hills and through the valleys. But they pass through the high hills. They just go along the stretch of the high hill. They do not go around, but they go over sometimes.

Allen Kapolak, 1998

Caribou eat many different kinds of plants, depending on availability and the time of year. Caribou seem to know what types of vegetation are rich in nutrients, and this enables calves to grow quickly and caribou to store backfat for the coming winter. One way to tell what a caribou has eaten is to examine the stomach contents. There are also signs on the land, such as caribou pellets (feces), snagged fur caught on bushes, or a branch that has been browsed at places where caribou have been eating.

During the Hiukkittaak Elder-Youth Camp, several elders showed the young people how to identify what caribou eat by opening up the stomachs and looking inside. Caribou like to eat dwarf birch, willows, and mountain avens. Elder Bessie Omilgoitok demonstrated how caribou eat *avaalaqiaq*, dwarf birch, by stripping the leaves from the branches with her teeth as a caribou would.

Forage Preferred by Caribou

> People know what caribou eat from the contents of the stomach and from how the meat tastes. When you are butchering a caribou, you look in the stomach and you can recognize pieces of tundra plants that are partly digested. This is one way to tell what kinds of vegetation caribou like to eat. Another way is to notice the changes in how the meat tastes during the different seasons. Caribou taste like grass in the summer.
>
> *Allen Kapolak, 1998*

> I have seen little white plants in the stomach. You can see the buds from willows too. They eat the little white plants and buds off the willows and other plants.
>
> *Connie Nalvana, 1999*

> In the spring, when the willows are moist and sprouting, they would loosen them with their snout. Then they would start gaining weight.... Caribou mostly eat lichen in the spring. Their stomachs are always full of

MARY KANIAK SHOWS PITIK NIPTANATIAK AND OVIK AKOLUK HOW TO MAKE A MATTRESS FROM WILLOW. HIUKKITTAAK ELDER-YOUTH CAMP, 1998.

lichen.… They eat a mixture of plants during the summer. Whatever sprouts, they will eat. In the fall, they will eat lichen. In the winter and fall, they eat lichen and grass. When the plants are dead, they look around for what they like to eat.

Mary Kaniak, 1998

When the vegetation starts to sprout, they will eat it. Whatever. Grasses … when they turn green … they eat off the land. Even willows. They even eat moist mud.

Bessie Omilgoitok, 1998

[Caribou eat] damp moss and willows.… I have seen pebbles in the stomach of caribou with a mixture of moss and grass.

John Akana, 1998

Moss and grass are their food. They eat grass as well as moss, lichen. [Caribou] are usually down low, where there is vegetation.

Allen Kapolak, 1998

They eat grass as well.… They eat grass and during the winter, they eat moss. They eat wood as well.

Paul Omilgoitok, 1998

MUSHROOMS   Caribou are fond of *kaiptauyat*, mushrooms. Jack Alonak (1998) explained that mushrooms are like a caribou water bottle, in that caribou eat and suck on mushrooms to keep their mouth moist on warm days. He compared mushrooms to caribou "snuff" that is chewed all day long.

Caribou usually dig out [mushrooms] with their hooves in flat areas of the land. They would look and spot them, even when they are frozen. That is what they eat. They can smell it.… They smell it through the snow and dig for it.

Archie Komak, 1998

You can tell [that caribou have been eating mush-
rooms] when the mushrooms have been peeled.
You can tell caribou have been eating there.

John Akana, 1998

Around August they tend to start to find mushrooms
in the stomach contents.... There has got to be a half a
dozen or so types of mushrooms that grow on the tundra. Caribou eat two types. Maybe you have seen those
ones with the really smooth top. Some of those that
get really big, they feed on those, and some of those
little ones with red on top, red coloured on top and sort
of mesh in the bottom, just like a cone on the bottom.
They have those ones also.

Bobby Algona, 1999

The availability and quality of vegetation drive caribou to migrate, calve, and
forage in certain areas. Differences in the tundra vegetation affect where caribou go and how long they stay in one area. Caribou go where the food is good;
and good food means good habitat.

135

10 Calving

Caribou are like people in that they have a natural urge to produce young in order for their kind to continue. According to the living memory of elders and stories told by those who have passed on, caribou have always followed a predictable yearly cycle. This cycle includes mating and calving periods that occur during annual migrations from southern wintering grounds to northern calving grounds and back again.

MARGO KADLUN-JONES AND
HER DAUGHTER, CALEY,
IKALUKTUUTTIAK, 1999.

RUTTING
SEASON

The rut begins in mid-October, when the caribou are at their healthiest after a summer of grazing and, hopefully, storing backfat. The cows are pregnant during their fall migration to the southern wintering grounds, into the winter months, and throughout their return migration to the north in mid-April. Cows and bulls typically travel separately, except when they are rutting.

Cows and bulls unite in the early fall to mate. The bulls make really loud snorting noises while they rut, and sometimes they fight for a cow or a group of cows. One might hear the rut from a great distance, not only because of the snorting, but also because the antlers of the fighting bulls knock together "as loud as thunder." While the older caribou are in rut, the calves, yearlings, and barren cows stay a short distance from the mating caribou.

It can be dangerous to be around caribou, especially the aggressive bulls, while they are in rut. This and the fact that people today do not like the musky taste of bulls during the rut means that there is little point in going out to hunt them during this time.

[The cows and bulls] would usually get together in October to mate. There would be many when they get together in October. They probably stay together for a month. That is the only time they would be together. The bulls would go their own way in November. They usually gather in October.

Charlie Keyok, 1998

> [During the rut], the yearlings and calves prefer to
> stay with the cows that are called *nurraittut* [cows
> without calves].
>
> *John Akana, 1998*

Before calving begins, the caribou have usually migrated from their southern wintering grounds. Starting in mid-April, pregnant cows along with yearlings lead the way to the calving grounds. Bulls follow the cows at a considerable distance. Hunters identify the pregnant cows by their large middle sections. Some hunters avoid shooting the pregnant cows if barren cows or bulls are readily available or if they do not like to eat the foetus. Qitirmiut today do not enjoy caribou foetus as much as in the past, although this varies within families and communities.

Cows normally give birth when the snow is melting and tundra plants are growing, usually between late May and mid-June. Some cows have been known to calve in April during years when the melt came particularly early. At the calving grounds, the calves learn by watching the cows and experimenting on their own how to feed on the rich and abundant tundra and, later, how to migrate southwards as the fall rut begins again.

In the spring, the people know when they are about to calve, when the cow is about to have the calf. They are usually about two years old when they calve. They have calves every year, once a year, every June.

Jimmy Maniyogina, 1999

I have seen caribou calving at the mainland. The calves would run around in a matter of minutes. I used to watch them.

Mackie Kaosoni, 1998

It was just born and it was still wet. We were holding it and it kept following us.... The mom was right beside us.

Martha Akoluk, 1998

The caribou are born during the spring and it does not take them long to become adults. Sometimes there are a lot of calves.... They would return to the calving grounds to calve themselves.... Some cows would have their calves late. When calves are born when the weather is warm, they have a better chance of survival.

Archie Komak, 1998

When they calve for the first time they are three years old.... I have never seen one before, but I have seen one about to give birth at the mainland. It was crouched on the ground, not afraid of my presence, because it was about to give birth. I just ignored it and left it as it was.

Frank Analok, 1999

I am not sure how old the cows are when they calve; they are not all the same.... I am not sure how many years later, but they are the same as humans, like women do not have babies after they have reached a certain age, that is how it is with caribou as well.

Archie Komak, 1998

Cows are very restless just before they lie down to give birth. They can go into labour while on the move and before reaching the more popular calving grounds. When this happens, the mother and calf take a short rest, then continue with the herd until they reach their destination at the calving grounds (see MAP 5).

Sometimes they would calve during their migration.

Moses Koihok, 1998

The caribou are constantly walking, calving, and they never stop.

Jessie Hagialok, 1998

Since Qitirmiut traditionally did not live at or near the calving grounds but rather set up camps along the caribou migration routes, most people have not actually seen a calf born. People have seen calves shortly after they have been born, but very few have been fortunate enough to see cows while they were giving birth. It is tradition to respect the calving period as a sacred time when the caribou should be left alone. Still, some say that the calving period is a good time to go hunting.

When the caribou cannot go any more or maybe when they are in pain, [they calve]. I heard from people, over in the Bathurst Inlet area, that that is when they go hunting. Only heard that one story. That is it.

George Kavanna, 1998

AFTER CALVING   Although caribou start moving around shortly after calving, there are frequent rest breaks for the calves, and the group moves slowly while feeding and looking for predators. Calves start to walk soon after they are born and quickly learn to find their mother's milk and tundra plants so as to gain weight, strength, and stamina. Qitirmiut say calves are smart because they are able to migrate so soon after being born.

They would go to the Bathurst Inlet area to calve. They would stop in one area in June, wait until the calves are strong enough, then they would go towards the wind when there are too many mosquitoes.

Moses Koihok, 1998

When a calf is born, they will wait till the fur is dry enough and then they will move on.

Mary Kaniak, 1998

When they are heading north, that is where they stop to calve. As they are walking and the calf is about to be born, that is where they are born. They can calve anywhere because they do not stop as they are walking. The calves usually start running as soon as they are born.

May Algona, 1999

Lots of caribou, after they have calved, head inland. They probably do not walk as much after they have calved. They probably do not walk as much when they are calving.

John Akana, 1998

When the caribou are finished at the calving grounds and they are heading south, they travel around. When the cows take a rest, the calves just go around and around their mother, playing around.... Newborn calves would walk side by side the yearlings. They would walk slowly with their calves. The cows would crouch and rest while the calves would run around them. They are so full of energy!

Paul Omilgoitok, 1998

Like all other animals, caribou have a strong instinct to continue their kind. This begins with the fall rut and continues as the cows lead the way northwards to the calving grounds. Although Qitirmiut respect and try not to bother caribou during their calving period, cows have occasionally calved close to Qitirmiut camps or communities. In these rare years, the proximity of the calving grounds has enabled people to watch the natural wonder of a cow giving birth or a young calf taking its first tentative steps. Nobody who has had the good fortune to experience these powerful moments is left untouched. Such observations strengthen the connections between Qitirmiut and caribou.

11 Calving Grounds

Various Qitirmiut think differently about how, why, and where cows choose their calving grounds. Some people shrugged their shoulders and did not want to hazard a guess. Other people suggested that the tundra was all the same and it depended on when the cows started moving northwards and how far they were physically able to travel before giving birth. This large-scale view differed from the more localized view of several people who explained that calving-ground selection had to do with such basics as the nuna, the hila, safety from predators, human activity, and particular snow conditions. Still others suggested that cows simply return to where they were born in order to calve.

Qitirmiut generally respect the calving period as a sensitive time for caribou and so choose to remain distant. Some seek out the calving grounds to harvest calf skins for clothing. Some years, the calving grounds may be too far to visit given the deteriorating snow conditions, and sightings of calving grounds are more common during years when the cows calve close to communities. Most Qitirmiut have not seen a calving ground before, so to describe what a calving ground might look like requires a person to think like a caribou.

> I have never been to a calving ground. It would be nice to
> see.… I can only assume that the place is basically… about
> the same sort of a terrain as here but lots of lakes. There
> are lots of lakes up there too.… Probably for fresh water.
>
> *Naikak Hakongak, 1998*

What Makes Good Calving Grounds

Based on a general understanding of caribou behaviour and respect for caribou instinct, Qitirmiut offered that cows know to choose calving grounds that are rich in food, free of most ice and snow, and far from predators. These qualities are important to all caribou habitat, but are even more important during the calving period.

Rich Habitat

The tundra at a calving ground needs to be nutritious in order for the cows to feed their calves and for the calves to gain strength to make their first migration south. In addition, the new mothers need to regain their strength after migrating, calving, and nursing.

> The cows usually go where there is food. They know
> where there is grass for their young ones. They have
> to find a right spot for their young ones.
>
> *Mary Kaniak, 1998*

> [Vegetation at a calving ground] is probably a little
> more rich.… Maybe it is exposed earlier in the spring
> so that it has time to grow. Maybe that is what it is.
> They find a spot where the snow goes the soonest, the

vegetation grows quicker maybe. That could be one of the places that they find that they go back to year after year 'cause they know it is going to be rich with food.… I think the food would have to be a bit richer because the calves need to grow quickly 'cause they start walking soon after they are born, but they need to get all the nutrients in as fast as they can before the fall or winter set in. It is going to be a long winter, so what they eat probably has to be a little bit richer than what they normally eat.

Naikak Hakongak, 1998

During the Hiukkittaak Elder-Youth Camp, a few elders observed that, after milk, cottongrass is the first food eaten by calves. This suggests that calving grounds are often located in areas where this plant is plentiful.

In addition to habitat, hila is a key factor for cows selecting where to calve. Areas that become snow-free first in the spring support tundra plants that have had more exposure to the sun and other growth factors. As such, the vegetation is typically rich with fresh shoots and new bark, both of which are preferred by caribou. To locate calving grounds, it may be that one must know which areas first become snow-free. At the same time, there can be small patches of snow nearby calving areas that provide relief from the heat.

FAVOURABLE CLIMATE, WEATHER, AND SNOW CONDITIONS

They calve when there is less snow, but there is still snow. Small patches, melting away.

Paul Omilgoitok, 1998

Changes in hila have brought warmer temperatures and led cows near water sources or moist areas in order to control their body temperature during calving. Calving grounds are rich in tundra vegetation not only as a food source, but also for shade to avoid warm summer temperatures.

Safety from predators is also a factor in where cows choose to calve. During the calving period, it is easy for wolves, bears, and other predators to hunt new caribou mothers and calves because they are so weak. These predators are smart, which is why they know to stalk an easy meal such as a calf. Caribou usually choose calving areas that are flat and open, so they can make an easy escape once they spot or smell a predator.

SAFE, FLAT TERRAIN

The cows are smart, they know what to do. Sometimes it is like they can talk when they have calves…. They would think of areas where there would be no wolves. They would go from one area to another, when there are many of them together. When there is a herd of them, they would go from one area to another, thinking of the safety of their calves, like taking care of them. Even if they are in one area, they would think of the wolves. That is why they are constantly moving. The cows would think of safety from wolves, but they can smell humans too.

Nellie Hikok, 1999

They are always on the flats, out in the open. They are always on flat land. In case there are wolves, they can escape into the water…. Cows usually calve on the flats, making it easier to escape from wolves. They are never in shaded areas.

Bessie Omilgoitok, 1998

As with consideration of how cows choose calving grounds, perspective matters when one talks about whether cows return to the "same" place to calve every year. From a broad perspective, Ahiarmiut cows return to the same northern calving grounds around Bathurst Inlet (see MAP 5, PAGE 179), while Kiillinik cows return to the same northern regions of Victoria Island. However, from a more localized viewpoint, exactly where the calving grounds are located changes slightly every year, depending on the combination of factors discussed earlier in this chapter.

On a large scale, there are many explanations for why caribou return to the "same" calving grounds each year. It might be that cows return to where they were born to calve or that they know where to go by sight and by their internal clocks. Perhaps caribou are like salmon in that they know how to return home to have their young. Maybe caribou have used the same calving grounds for generations and return instinctively to these same areas.

> Over in Kunayuk [Ellice River], the caribou always go by the same area all the time, by the river. They must calve somewhere up the river, because they always go the same way every year. Sometimes they are late, sometimes they are early.
>
> *George Kavanna, 1999*

> Older caribou must be used to [the calving grounds]. Recognize by sight.
>
> *George Kuptana, 1997*

> They return to their calving grounds like they always have. It is the same as birds, they return to their nesting grounds. The same holds true with all animals.… Yeah, they return to the grounds they were born on. They go to the same area to calve, like they always have.
>
> *Frank Analok, 1999*

> I think [the cows] probably return to the same spot where they were born [to have their calves]. Maybe like the Arctic tern, they just go back.
>
> *Naikak Hakongak, 1998*

> That is where they always calved every year…. Yeah,
> they always return to their birthplace to calve. Because
> it is their land…. They would go to a spot where there
> are no caribou, on their own to calve.
>
> *Charlie Keyok, 1998*

On a smaller scale, it may be that cows decide where to calve depending on the type or condition of the tundra. Caribou herds can break apart to avoid land that is overgrazed and trampled and, in doing so, select very different calving areas every year. For the Ahiarmiut caribou, these areas are continually shifting around the Bathurst Inlet.

> They do not always calve in the same area that they
> have calved previously at.
>
> *Moses Koihok, 1998*

> They would calve in different areas than the years
> before. That is how it is, that is how they are. It is [the]
> same as the environment, always changing.
>
> *Moses Koihok, 1998*

> They probably scatter along the way and go to differ-
> ent places. The survival rate is higher…. So there is got
> to be some different areas along this side of the
> Bathurst Inlet, both sides of the Bathurst Inlet that
> they calve on. 'Cause you can see there [are] some
> areas that are fairly flat, and maybe they go to differ-
> ent ones and even on the other side around the Arctic
> Sound areas as well.
>
> *Naikak Hakongak, 1998*

Calving Ground Locations   Stories about the locations of calving grounds have been passed from one generation to the next. For the TNP, several elders and hunters marked out these traditional calving areas, as shown on MAP 5 (see PAGE 179). At least three factors contribute to why many calving areas remain unmarked. First, people were hesitant to mark areas when they were not entirely sure of the boundaries of the calving grounds. They preferred not to make any marks than to be inaccurate in presenting their knowledge.

> I am not too familiar with calving grounds, so I do not want to indicate any area that I do not know about. I do not want to mention anything that I do not know about.
>
> *John Akana, 1998*

Second, many elders do not feel comfortable reading maps or seeing them as a representation of reality. Third, it was unrealistic to interview everybody in all communities who knew calving-ground locations. Unfortunately, many grounds were missed, which means that this map is but a sample of calving areas and should only be used as a general guide.

In general, calving grounds for the Ahiarmiut caribou are found either east, west, or south of the Bathurst Inlet. Traditional calving grounds were identified as being nearby the Hiukkittaak River, Katimanik, Hanningayuk, Tahikaffaluk, and Tahikyoak, as well as near the community of Kingauk. The calving grounds for the Kiillinik caribou are outside the study area of the TNP.

> This is where we watched caribou calving [Hanningayuk]. We would watch. It was fun! They would calve all over this area. But this is where we watched them calve one spring. We watched quite a bit.… They always calve around here. This is where they would calve too, in June. They calve in June. But that is where we have seen most. Calves would be born here.
>
> *May Algona, 1999*

TO ACKNOWLEDGE THAT NOBODY KNOWS THE WAYS OF THE CARIBOU IS AN EXPRESSION OF RESPECT AS WELL AS RECOGNITION THAT PEOPLE DO NOT KNOW EVERYTHING ABOUT THE WORLD OR ABOUT CARIBOU.

PAUL OMILGOITOK AND HIS SON, MEYOK, DISCUSS CALVING GROUNDS, IKALUKTUUTTIAK, 1998.

151

They must calve around here, around this area [east of Hiukkittaak River]. While they were walking in this area, [Henry] Kamoayok and I used to try catching them. Cannot grab.... Caribou calving grounds. That happens there every June. From June to August. 1945 maybe.... At Kuukkiviagyuk.

Paul Omilgoitok, 1998

There are always a lot of calves there. It must be a calving ground.... It is further inland, on the other side. We spent one spring at Aniaghiugvik [Fishing Creek], and caribou were calving there.

Bessie Omilgoitok, 1998

Last year, though, Angivrana saw a whole bunch calving by Tikikvik [west of Bathurst Inlet, along the Burnside River] when he went by helicopter.... A couple years back, I have seen calves being born around Elliot Point or Fishing Creek. I have seen newborns around there. Also at Hanningayuk. I had camps there during the summer and winters.... There were many wolves around there too.

Jessie Hagialok, 1998

I have never seen caribou calving anywhere else, just in the Bathurst Inlet area, Hanningayuk and Tahikyoak. Here are the calving grounds.

Nellie Hikok, 1999

[Here] are calving areas, just near Young Point, behind that point.... About ten years ago they were calving right in here around this area [near Bathurst Inlet community] in the spring till mid-June, early June. I saw them just as they were born. Just come out. Maybe a couple of hours old.

Allen Kapolak, 1998

I have seen one calf being born here. I was following them one spring, in April. I have seen only one giving birth there. It gave birth as it was running away. But I have seen three born here at Kaumaugaktuk [Rocking Horse Lake].

Connie Nalvana, 1999

It was around Tahikaffaluk and Tahikyoak. At these areas, I have seen calves being born.... I do not know if the [calving grounds] have changed, but we will see that when we do not see them as much.... I am just wondering where they will calve next. We will find out soon.

George Kuptana, 1998

From the 1970s to the mid-1990s, the Ahiarmiut caribou calved on the east side of Bathurst Inlet, but they shifted to the west side for the latter half of the 1990s. Calving-ground locations have generally shifted back and forth from the east to west side of Bathurst Inlet depending on human activity, the timing of the season, and the effects of hila on nuna. Some years, calving occurs south of Bathurst Inlet.

SHIFTS IN CALVING GROUNDS

Last year we were flying in the helicopter and saw a lot of calves round the Hood River. Last few years I think they have been calving around the Hood: 1996, 1997, and 1995. They starting calving on the west side probably about five years ago now, five or six years ago.

Allen Kapolak, 1998

The caribou usually have their young on the other side [east side of Bathurst Inlet] and around Beechey Lake from what I know. Around Beechey Lake, Umingmaktuuk, and the Brown Sound areas.

Doris Kingnektak, 1998

When they come late from the south, they go to calve there [west side of Bathurst Inlet]. They would stay on that side [west] if they come late in the spring.

Mary Kaniak, 1998

The ones that come late from the south have gone there [west side of Bathurst Inlet] for the past two years.

John Akana, 1998

They used to calve around here [east of Bathurst Inlet], but now they calve over here [west of Bathurst Inlet]. They used to calve on this side of Tahikaffaaluk Lake by Kunayuk. They calve here by Kunayuk; they used to calve around here. Right now they calve somewhere else. That is where they have always calved, since the past. They used to go close to Kingauk.... Around here was the first time I saw a caribou with a calf. A long time ago ... maybe 1950.... I have heard in the recent years of a lot of caribou calving around here. Just a few years ago, a couple of years, I heard of caribou calving here. I must have been around sixty or fifty-nine years old. Probably 1966, I have heard of caribou calving [west of Arctic Sound at Tikigakyok].... Yes, always the same place they go to calve.... I have heard of caribou calving on this side of Bathurst Inlet, in front of Kitunnik, last year and the year before. There has been the most caribou here in the last few years.

John Akana, 1998

LENA KAMOAYOK, PITOKIK, 1997.

Knowledge of the exact location of calving grounds is not so critical to Qitirmiut as it was in the past. However, because of their respect for caribou and for their homeland, and especially in light of northern development and recent climate change, people continue to monitor the places where caribou choose to give birth.

12 Caribou and Our Warming Climate

For generations, Qitirmiut have observed correlations between hila, nuna, and caribou that have enabled them to survive in a harsh environment. These relationships are changing, however, due to a combination of earlier spring melt and later fall freeze-up. Higher temperatures have led to a longer period of summer-like conditions, particularly in the past five years. This window of warmer and longer days has influenced caribou migrations, the body condition of the animals, and their population levels.

Changes Observed in the Weather

Weather, it is hard to say, but I find the weather from long ago is getting hotter, getting hotter every year. I noticed the weather is getting warmer and hotter from long time ago.

George Kavanna, 1998

Everything is changing. It is not the same as before. Sometimes it does not snow as much as it used to. It never gets as cold as it used to. A long time ago, when the weather got bitterly cold, the fuels like heating oil, gasoline, and naphtha used to freeze.... It used to get real cold in the past, but nowadays it is not the same.

May Algona 1999

It was so much warmer the last few years, in the 1990s and the late 1980s.

Bobby Algona, 1999

The warmer temperatures that were common in the 1990s affect snow and ice conditions. Safe and fruitful hunting, fishing, and sealing require careful observation of ice thickness, snow patchiness, melting rates and patterns, and changes both within and between the layers of snow and ice. These observations have always guided Qitirmiut to safe and expedient travel routes, for example, where the ice is thick enough to support a heavy sled. In the past, Qitirmiut living off the land had to watch carefully when and how the ice melted and froze. Although Qitirmiut no longer live off the land in the same way as they did traditionally, such pastimes as hunting and fishing remain important and still require careful observations of ice and snow conditions during spring melt and fall freeze-up.

SPRING ARRIVES EARLIER

Spring melt of snow and ice seems to be coming earlier, and fall freeze-up is much later than people remember from the days of their youth.

The weather is warmer now ... the snow seems to go earlier in the late spring.

Archie Komak, 1998

Some Qitirmiut we interviewed thought that spring is actually coming later now. These comments came from the eldest interviewees, who do not spend a great amount of time on the land any more.

> Right now [1997], it has not started to warm up yet. It seems to come later.
>
> *George Kuptana, 1997*

> The weather has changed too. It is not hard to tell. The usual time spring comes around seems to come later.... Things have changed from a long time ago.... Nowadays it is different. Even the land is different. That is what the people from Iqaluit were saying last year [1998].
>
> *Frank Analok, 1999*

In addition to spring arriving earlier these days, fall comes later. Before temperatures started to warm, freeze-up began in the late summer, during August or September. In the late 1990s, the ice started to freeze in October or November.

FALL ARRIVES LATER

> Nowadays freeze-up occurs in November. Sometimes there would be no ice at all, and other times it would go again after freezing up. It has changed. In the past, the ocean would be completely frozen over in November.
>
> *Frank Analok, 1999*

> It seems to be getting warmer. The ocean freezes over later than usual.
>
> *John Akana, 1998*

> Sometimes in the late summer, years ago, it would freeze up. Now it seems to freeze up late, and other times it would freeze up earlier. Sometimes it would freeze up late. That is how it is.... This happened for many years. A long time ago the ice on the ocean used to go away late [in the spring]. Nowadays it goes earlier, so waiting is not so bad any more.
>
> *Archie Komak, 1998*

The combination of an earlier spring and a later fall has led to longer periods of summerlike conditions in recent years, which influence the environment and caribou. For example, leads in the ice opened earlier, vegetation was more rich and abundant, ice was thinner, and water levels fell. There were also more days of extreme heat and sporadic freeze-thaw cycles. These impacts from a warming climate affect caribou movements and migrations, population levels, overall health, survival, and behaviour.

Migration routes and locations of calving grounds have shifted on a local scale partially because of the impacts of a warming climate. Patches of water opened earlier in ice on the sea, rivers, and lakes, forcing caribou to change their normal migration routes. Plants became taller, bushier, and more plentiful, and as a result, caribou shifted their migration routes towards these areas of rich vegetation.

With warmer temperatures, there are changes in tundra plants that caribou either eat or use for shade. Plants are larger and there are more of them, particularly shrubs, in certain traditional camping areas such as the Hiukkittaak River. The number of different types of tundra plants has also increased, especially on Kiillinik. Recently, there have been some types of lichens and flowering plants on Kiillinik that have never been seen there before.

Nowadays I see more willows when I am walking around. Sometimes I would pick willows. I never used to see any willows when we first moved [to Ikaluktuuttiak]. I would pick some willows to cook with out on the land in the summer, when they have grown.

Bessie Omilgoitok, 1998

NELLIE HIKOK AND SANDRA EYEGETOK, KUGLUKTUK, 1999.

Today there is growth on the land. The land is changing, that is why on [Victoria] Island there is more growth.... There was no vegetation around here. There was only gravel and pebbles long ago. Nowadays it seems to be continuing to get more vegetation and because of this, the land is getting beautiful.... It is the first time I have started to see them, now for about three years, they are growing. Just like the mainland, there is more vegetation growing … the island is getting prettier when it grows. There seems to be more grass too. It used to be only sand, only mud.

Moses Koihok, 1998

During the Hiukkittaak Elder-Youth Camp, many elders commented on how some plants near the shores of rivers have grown taller and more lush than they remembered seeing in the 1930s and 1940s. Willows and alders throughout the Bathurst Inlet region grow taller, have thicker stems, and produce more branches than they remembered during years that they travelled with their parents and as young adults.

There was no vegetation around [Ikaluktuuttiak]…. There is more vegetation growing now along the shoreline.

Moses Koihok, 1998

Given that vegetation has grown larger, especially near the shoreline, and that caribou are often found in shaded places, it is possible that caribou have shifted their migration routes to seek out these areas. This may be happening at least on a small scale.

The warming climate in the 1990s and the resulting changes in water, ice, and snow definitely caused caribou to shift their migration routes. There were differences in the timing and manner that ice melted, and in the levels of bodies of water that caribou had to cross.

CHANGES IN WATER, ICE, AND SNOW

ELLA PANEGYUK, HIUKKITTAAK, 1999.

Warmer spring temperatures combined with currents cause the ice to melt earlier, creating patches of open water known as "leads." These leads force caribou to alter their spring and fall migrations across sea ice. For example, if a lead is too wide to swim across, caribou may turn around and go back to shore or follow the lead until they find an area where the ice is thick enough to continue. Sometimes caribou swim across leads if the open water stretches from the ice edge to the shore. Otherwise, caribou rarely swim across leads because it is difficult for them to get back out of the water and onto the ice. When leads are especially wide, caribou have to change their migration routes.

> [The caribou] mainly come through there [across from Elliot Point in southern Bathurst Inlet] when they are calving on the east side. For some caribou, it is still the same…. The caribou … come around through from Portage Bay off Kuadjuk Island…. They come south then go around again. They cannot hit that open water down there…. That open water has always been the same … [but] it opens earlier and way bigger [nowadays].
>
> *Allen Kapolak, 1998*

When rivers melt earlier than usual, they can flow with such speed and force that they can be difficult for caribou to cross. In addition, ice floating downstream can be dangerous.

> Generally, [the caribou] have been staying to the west. Only a few coming through last few years, mostly staying around the west. Maybe it is because the Hood and Bathurst Rivers started to go earlier and they have a hard time getting across. All the rivers. Warmer weather these past few years.
>
> *George Kapolak Haniliak, 1998*

JESSIE HAGIALOK, KINGAUK, 1998.

Qitirmiut are experts in noticing which leads open up and which rivers melt first and how these leads can change location throughout the melting period from one year to the next. For example, certain places in Elu Inlet and Bathurst Inlet are extremely dangerous during the spring, fall, and winter because of ocean currents that make it difficult to judge the ice thickness and due to open water that is found year-round.

In the 1990s, warmer temperatures, a longer ice-free period, and shorter winters meant that ice on lakes, rivers, and the sea did not have as much time to become as thick as it was in the past.

> Nowadays it freezes up later than usual. It does not get thick as it used to.
>
> *Buster Kailik, 1998*

> It does not get as cold as it used to. A long time ago it would be bitter cold and the ice would be thicker.... The water gets warm now and takes longer to freeze.... The ice does not get as thick as it used to, maybe because the water is warmer than it used to be … [My] brother was sealing one day and said "Sis, come and see this. The ice is thinning. It is not even spring yet and it is thin."…. The ice does not get as thick as it used to…. Some of the younger people have mentioned that as well.
>
> *Connie Nalvana, 1998*

Thinner ice can cause problems for caribou, since they need a certain ice thickness in order to travel across frozen bodies of water, especially in the southern Bathurst Inlet area. While the warmth of the sun, the length of daylight, and the timing of the season may trigger caribou to cross over a frozen lake, river, or ocean, the ice may not be thick enough to support their weight. During the fall, the ice must be thick enough for caribou to cross during their migration southwards towards their wintering grounds. Similarly, in the spring, the ice must be thick enough for caribou to cross during the migrations northwards towards their calving grounds. If the ice is thin or there is open water, caribou will usually change their migration routes by walking alongside the lead for several kilometres, thereby wasting valuable energy. Sometimes caribou will cross over the thin ice, fall through, and die of hypothermia.

> Last year I noticed the ice close fairly late from the years before. That is when a few caribou were trying to cross from Cape Peel, on Kiillinik. I heard from the guys that were working from the North Warning System that some caribou drowned near Cape Peel, about seventy miles west from Ikaluktuuttiak. They were trying to migrate across towards Surrey Lake and Ikaluktuuk, come towards Ikaluktuuttiak area. I heard not lots drowned but … less than a hundred, I think.
>
> *George Kavanna, 1998*

Several Qitirmiut observed an increase in the number of caribou drowning because of thinner ice in the 1990s. While travelling by snowmobile in 1996, two community members found themselves amid hundreds of antlers that were frozen and sticking out of the ice like an antler forest.

HIGHER WATER
LEVELS AND
LOWER SHORELINES

In addition to changes in ice thickness, water levels around Bathurst Inlet seem to have dropped. This influences the shoreline, which provides important caribou habitat.

> The water level seems to be getting lower.… In the past, the water levels were higher. Some of the rivers have gone.… During the summer, in August, people travelling by boat have noticed that the water level has dropped compared to the past. People liked the water levels of the rivers and ocean then. The islands on the ocean seem to be getting bigger than they used to be. Kanuyauyaq, an elder, used to say the rocks barely showed back then. Now the islands seem longer, higher, and bigger.
>
> *John Akana, 1998*

The water level seems to have gone down in the lakes, and the rivers do not flow as strong as they used to. The lakes seem to dry out too.... I wonder why that is happening. Does anybody know why that is happening? That was starting to happen at Contwoyto Lake when we moved.

May Algona, 1999

It seems that the weather has changed.... The water level seems to have dropped. It seems like there is less water. The lakes seem to be smaller and dry out. That is what we have noticed.

Annie Kaosoni, 1998

> The shoreline is now lower than it used to be. It is
> changed. Even the ocean. Maybe the land is getting
> higher. The shorelines used to be a lot higher.... The
> shorelines have changed, continue to change....
> The shoreline today is lower than when I was a boy,
> unless the land has got higher.
>
> *Moses Koihok, 1998*

While water levels have dropped, there has also been more snow in some places. Since the weather is warmer in the summer, the water is evaporating, as evidenced by more thunderstorms and lightning.

> It seems to snow more now in the spring. When the
> snow is melting, the water, it gets higher. Sometimes
> there is a lot of water when the weather gets warm.
> When it has snowed a lot during the year.
>
> *Paul Omilgoitok, 1999*

MORE INSECTS   Besides changes in the seasons, in the tundra, and in water, ice, and snow conditions, another way warmer temperatures and a longer period of summerlike conditions influence caribou is that there are more bugs. Recently, there have been "hot hot" and "humid summers," which have made the land "drier" and brought more bugs, especially mosquitoes.

> There were not many mosquitoes back then [in the
> 1970s]. They would only be around for a short time.
>
> *Frank Analok, 1998*

As the temperature increases, so does the number of mosquitoes, but at some point it is too hot for mosquitoes to survive. During the 1998 summer, temperatures rose so high that the mosquitoes were a problem for only one week. Usually the bugs are bad for two weeks starting in late June or early July.

> When there are too many mosquitoes, [caribou] would
> gather and go in circles to get rid of the mosquitoes.
> Sometimes when they shook the flies off, it would

make the sound like thunder. There would be so many mosquitoes that they would look like snowflakes. You can see even from a distance. Even from a distance you can hear the noise they make when they shake the mosquitoes off. That is what has been told.... After they have calved, there are too many mosquitoes.

Moses Koihok, 1998

Caribou can overheat and lose weight on hot and windless days while running around to escape excessive swarms of mosquitoes and not eating. Caribou may not survive the winter if they lose too much fat.

Sometimes [caribou] would freeze when they are skinny. The female and calf would freeze while they are swimming to another location ... on their route.

George Kuptana, 1997

In addition to noticing the warmer temperatures in the 1990s, Qitirmiut find it more difficult to plan for the weather because it has become so unpredictable and variable. Today, people understand weather less, as they are not outside and living in it as much. Still, weather events seem to be beyond the realm of expectation or what people consider normal. Nowadays there are more cases of freezing rain and sporadic freeze-thaw cycles that lock vegetation in frozen sleet and make it impossible for caribou to eat. This can cause caribou to starve to death. Days of extreme heat were also more common in the 1990s, when caribou can become overheated, exhausted, and skinny. Combined, these exteme weather conditions could lead to lower caribou population levels.

Unpredictable and Variable Weather

Back in the 1960s I could almost say that I could predict the weather any day, whereas nowadays you might think it is going to rain ... or snow back then, but today there is nothing. Turn back and no [snow] dump.... That is the big difference from the 1960s and today.... Everybody that I talked to said that they could predict the weather in the 1960s. It is more predictable and stable, whereas nowadays it is unstable.... [There is]

Mackie Kaosoni,
Uvayuq, 1999.

any kind of weather on any day. You can have rain in February sometimes nowadays. Or snow in August. Hail in August. Hail or even snow in July! I can remember … six or seven years ago, we had a snow-bank outside my door in August. That one night it really snowed and froze and big snow piled outside my tent in August. About seven years ago, I think it was, … and next day it was all gone again.

Bobby Algona, 1999

You never know the weather.… It is a fact that the weather is never the same.… Every year is always different.… Everything is always changing. Right now it seems to be getting worse. That I have noticed in my lifetime. It used to get real nice outside when I was younger, right after a storm. Right now when the weather gets bad, it seems consistent. We do not know the weather. It has a caretaker of its own.

Frank Analok, 1997

When we moved here [Ikaluktuuttiak] in 1964, it would always be cold and foggy in the spring. It would never clear up. Nowadays it gets warm and does not get foggy as much.

Bessie Omilgoitok, 1998

The general trend of recent warmer temperatures has some people concerned because changes in the weather, environment, and wildlife populations seem to be happening too quickly for both people and the environment. This has resulted in extreme events or happenings that are beyond what is considered normal. Caribou are affected adversely by this unpredictable and variable weather, particularly by freeze-thaw cycles, hot days, more bugs, and smoky skies from forest fires.

FREEZE-THAW
CYCLES

In the 1990s, there were more short-term changes in temperature. At times, these fluctuations caused variable freeze-thaw cycles. These occurred when a few days of warm weather started to melt the ice and snow, then a sudden cold period followed. This warming then cooling trend caused the meltwater to freeze and form an icy layer on top of the snow or directly atop the tundra. These freeze-thaw cycles can happen in both the spring and fall, particularly during breakup and freeze-up. Alternatively, a spring blizzard can cover the ground with heavy snow.

> It has been melting sooner than usual, [and] then
> freezing again.... It has been melting and freezing.
>
> *Anonymous C, 1998*

Caribou numbers decrease during the years when there are many freeze-thaw cycles. These events trap lichen and other tundra plants in the ice and make them unavailable as forage. Thus, warmer temperatures and variable weather conditions may cause a decrease in caribou population levels due to starvation.

> The snow was covered in ice. It had rained after a big snowfall. That is when some of the caribou starved to death, but in another area of land, where it is not so rough, they were fine.... Some areas were fine where it did not rain.... The land was covered in sleet and ice, and some caribou and muskox froze to death. When the land is covered in ice, where it is not so rough, some caribou would freeze to death.
>
> *Archie Komak, 1998*

> One spring, a lot of caribou died because of freezing rain and sleet. There were no areas for them to feed around.... They had starved to death because of sleet. They had nowhere to eat. The ice was too thick.... They could not dig through it.
>
> *Moses Koihok 1998*

ANNIE KAOSONI,
UVAYUQ, 1999.

There were more hot days and days of record temperatures (over thirty degrees Celsius) in the 1990s than in previous decades. Temperatures were hot enough to melt the ice and snow in just a few short days, both in communities and out on the land.

HIGHER
TEMPERATURES

Few years ago, two years ago [1996], it was so hot in July … 40 degrees above.

Doris Kingnektak, 1998

Caribou would die from the heat of the sun. When the weather gets too hot, a lot of them would suffocate side by side. My wife and I have seen that at Tahialuk. They suffocated from the heat of the sun.

Mackie Kaosoni, 1998

When it gets too hot, the caribou would suffocate. When it gets too hot in the summer, because they are used to the bitter cold. Those that have suffocated would look like they have been shot down.

Annie Kaosoni, 1998

When caribou are exposed to extreme heat, people notice changes in their health and body condition. For example, caribou become skinnier and weaker. Caribou die when they get too skinny. In general, days of extreme heat, more common nowadays, are connected to decreases in caribou numbers. Hot temperatures alone can kill caribou. The associated increase in mosquitoes that harass caribou can also cause caribou to become exhausted from running around, to overheat, and eventually to die.

During the summer when there are a lot of mosquitoes in the warm weather, they would die of exhaustion … when the weather is too hot for them.

Bessie Angulalik, 1998

MARY KAOSONI,
IKALUTUUTTIAK, 1997.

ALICE KINGNEKTAK,
KAREN KAMOAYOK, AND
KOAHA KAKOLAK COLLECT
CAPELIN, HANIGAKHIK, 1997.

In the summer, sometimes the caribou get weak. They get really hot. Sometimes their meat goes green, especially around the haunches. You get some of the green meat from where they get too hot in the summer, so that you know not to eat that caribou…. And it gets too hot so that their meat goes strange and then it turns green.

Naikak Hakongak, 1998

Hot temperatures increase the number of forest fires and make the skies hazy, further contributing to caribou fatalities or breathing difficulties.

FOREST FIRES
AND SMOKY SKIES

From the smog, there were a lot of dead bulls on the land. It was really hot that time and some caribou had died.

Charlie Keyok, 1998

There is always smoke. When there are forest fires down south, it really gets smoky up here, and if it is foggy you could smell the smoke. Last year [1997] it was really smoggy. You could smell forest fires, maybe for at least five days, four or five days anyway. Somewhere there was a big forest fire, and it was a dry year for the Yellowknife area…. Probably [caribou were sensitive to smoke]. We were. We would go out and say, "So stink! Cover your nose and mouth!"

Anonymous C, 1998

During hot days, caribou have to try to keep cool so they do not overheat. As the climate generally warms and days of extreme heat and forest fires become more frequent, ways to prevent dehydration and overheating become more important for caribou. Caribou adapt to the heat by staying near the shorelines, lying on patches of snow, drinking water, wading and swimming in the water, eating moist plants, and sucking on mushrooms.

> When the weather is hot during the summer the caribou would have those [mushrooms] when they are thirsty.
>
> *Bessie Omilgoitok, 1998*

> [Mushrooms] are what the caribou use to keep their mouths moist when they walk. They need water and that is what they use when they are thirsty.... They would keep these mushrooms in their mouths because they are moist inside. Wet, really wet.
>
> *Jack Alonak, 1998*

MEYOK OMILGOITOK,
IKALUKTUUTTIAK, 1999.

Both caribou and Qitirmiut have been affected by a warming climate marked by unpredictable and variable weather. In the 1990s, Qitirmiut noticed ways in which caribou were affected by climate change. The combination of earlier spring breakup and later fall freeze-up has led to a longer period of summerlike conditions when there is no ice on the lakes, rivers, and ocean.

Qitirmiut have always connected weather patterns with wildlife activity and moon phases. Recently, they have had more difficulty making these connections due to unpredictable and variable weather. Extreme events such as high temperatures outside the realm of reasonable expectation are new to the region. Exactly how both Qitirmiut and caribou will adapt to this changing climate is yet to be seen.

13 Looking to the Future

Donna Tikhak,
Umingmaktuuk, 1998.

Through the TNP, Qitirmiut elders and hunters shared their experiences, observations, and explanations of caribou in the Bathurst Inlet area. In doing so, they revealed their special relationship with these animals and contributed to a new understanding of caribou that can guide current and future generations.

People listened to traditional knowledge. That is how they know everything.

Jimmy Maniyogina, 1998

I do not want to be the only person telling stories.… There are other elders that can talk about [caribou] as well. They can talk about what I have just mentioned or anything else they have in mind.

Frank Analok, 1999

People should help each other and feel free to voice their opinions. People should do all they can to protect our traditional land and water.

Moses Koihok, 1998

This account should be used together with the many accompanying maps and detailed transcripts compiled by the TNP and stored in a database that is selectively available through the Kitikmeot Heritage Society. This work is only the beginning of what could be documented, for example, about other animals or regions.

Written materials are only one means to learn from Qitirmiut, and as elders are quick to point out, one should learn by seeing, listening, experiencing, participating, and inquiring. Through this chronicle, Qitirmiut elders and hunters have presented insight into what is understood about caribou. We hope that future works will continue to contribute to this understanding.

I cannot think of anything else. I do not want to tell any lies.

Nellie Hikok, 1999

BUSTER KAILIK AND
CONNIE NALVANA,
KUGLUKTUK, 1999.

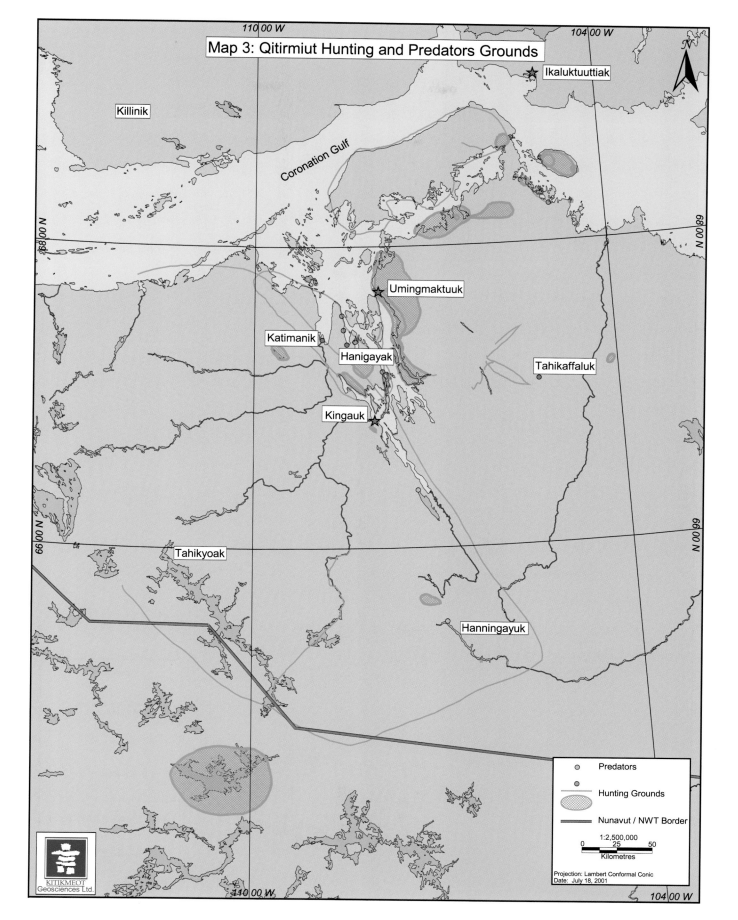

Map 3: Qitirmiut Hunting and Predators Grounds

Killinik

Coronation Gulf

Ikaluktuuttiak

Umingmaktuuk

Katimanik

Hanigayak

Tahikaffaluk

Kingauk

Tahikyoak

Hanningayuk

Predators

Hunting Grounds

Nunavut / NWT Border

1:2,500,000

0   25   50
Kilometres

Projection: Lambert Conformal Conic
Date: July 18, 2001

KITIKMEOT
Geosciences Ltd.

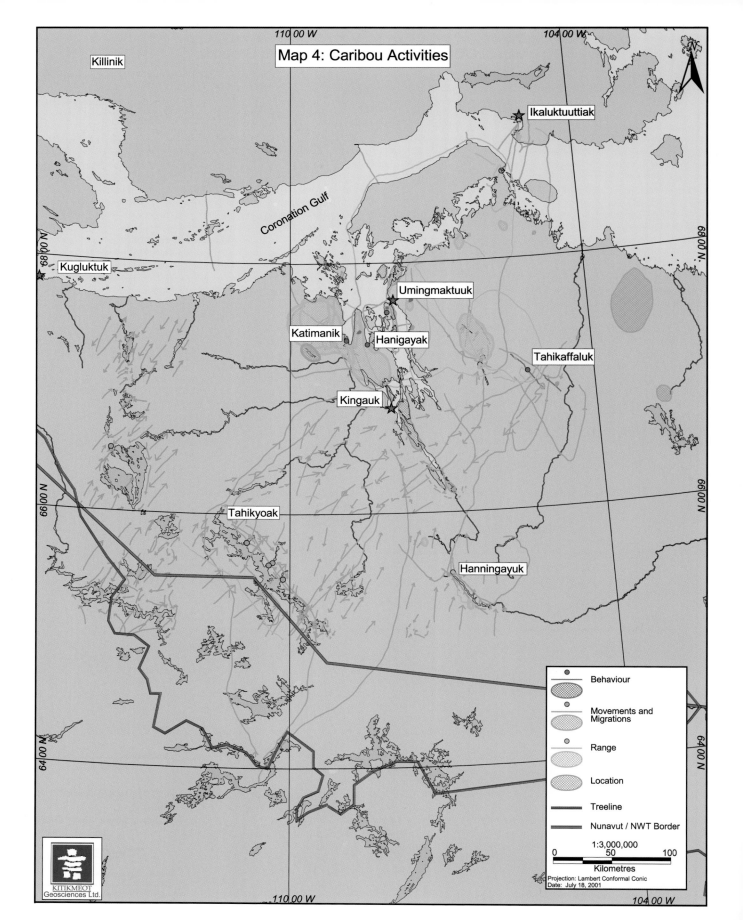

Map 4: Caribou Activities

Killinik

Ikaluktuuttiak

Coronation Gulf

Kugluktuk

Umingmaktuuk

Katimanik

Hanigayak

Tahikaffaluk

Kingauk

Tahikyoak

Hanningayuk

Behaviour

Movements and Migrations

Range

Location

Treeline

Nunavut / NWT Border

1:3,000,000

0   50   100

Kilometres

Projection: Lambert Conformal Conic
Date: July 18, 2001

KITIKMEOT
Geosciences Ltd.

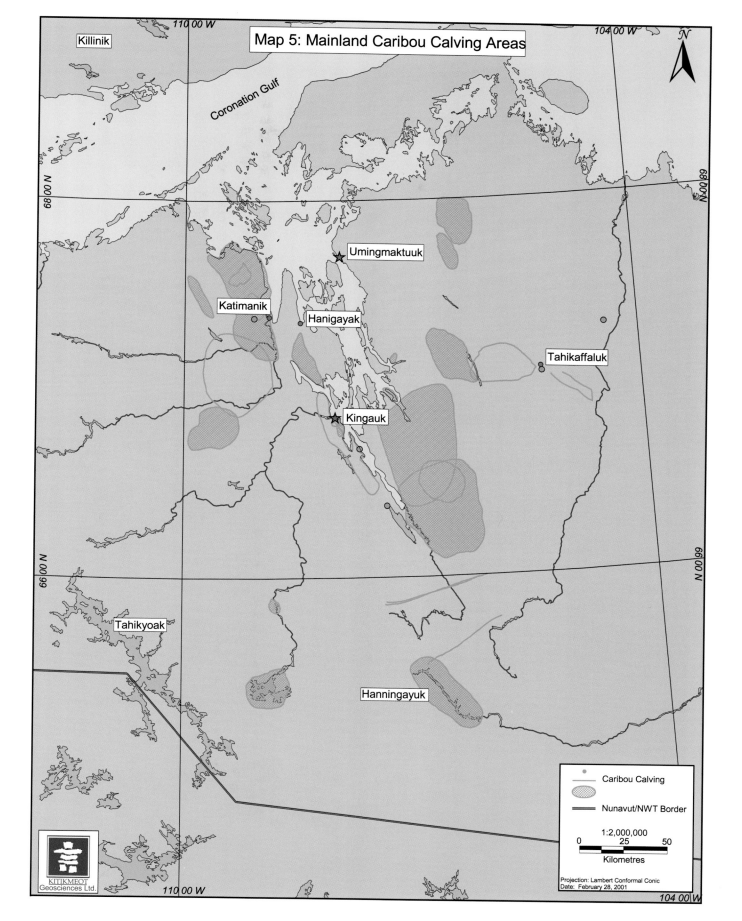

Map 5: Mainland Caribou Calving Areas

Killinik

Coronation Gulf

Umingmaktuuk

Katimanik

Hanigayak

Tahikaffaluk

Kingauk

Tahikyoak

Hanningayuk

KITIKMEOT
Geosciences Ltd.

Caribou Calving

Nunavut/NWT Border

1:2,000,000
0   25   50
Kilometres

Projection: Lambert Conformal Conic
Date: February 28, 2001

110 00 W

104 00 W

68 00 N

66 00 N

PAUL NICKLEN

Appendix A
Place Names of the Kitikmeot Region

Contributed by Gerry Atatahak, Sandra Eyegetok, Naikak Hakongak, Margo Kadlun-Jones, Doug Stern, and TNP interviewees. The last spelling is that of the new Inuinnaqtun system. In many cases, one name refers to several locations. Coordinates for the exact location of all places are noted in the TNP spatial database.

Traditional Place Name
Other Spellings
(other geographical references)

Aagiak
> Agiak
> Agiaq
> (Grays Bay)

Aghagak
> Aqhagaq
> (near Parry Bay)

Agvilikyuak
> Arvilikyuaq

Aimaukkattaak
> Aimaukataak
> Aimaukkattaak
> Aimaukkattaaq

Akiakokyoak
> Akiaokyoak
> Akiagokyoak

Akoglialok

Akiagoaluk Lake
> (Akigoyvaki)

Akullialuk

Akunik
> Akunnik
> Akunniq

Algaguhik
> Alraruhiq

Algak
> (island north of Hanigayak)

Amaaktuagyuk
> Amaaktuaryuk
> Amaaqtuaryuk

Amaaktuk
> Amaaqtuq

Amagoalgivik
> Amarualrivik

Amaloktuok
> Amaloktuok

Anamaloktok

Angmaluktuagyuk
> Angmaluqtuaryuk

Angmaluktuuk
> Anmaluktuuk
> Angmaluqtuuq

Aniaghiugvik
> Aniarhiurvik
> Aniaghiurvik
> Aniaqhiurvik
> (Fishing Creek, south of Kingauk)

Apaalik

Arin'ngaq

Arvilikyuaq
> Arvilikyuaq
> (the old name for Pelly Bay
> or Kuugaaruk)

Aulativik

Aulativikyoak
  Aulattivikyuaq
  (White Bear Point,
  east of Ellice River)

Avingak

Ayappappaktokvik
  Ayapaqpaqturvik
  (Burnside River)

Ekalivik
  Iqallivik

Ekaluktuuk
  Iqaluktuuq

Etibliakyok
  Itipliaryuk
  (isthmus of Kent Peninsula
  and mainland)

Hagvaktok
  Harvaqtuuq

Hanigaghiahugignik
  Haniriagutiiq
  Haniraghiahurirnik

Hanigakhik
  Haniraqhiq
  (Brown Sound)

Hanigayak
  Hanirakhik
  Hanirarhiq
  Hanirayaq

Hanikiagohik
  Haniraghiarahiq
  (Brown Sound)

Hanningayuk
  Haningayuk
  Hanningayuq
  (Beechey Lake)

Haoniktok
  Hauniktuuk
  Hauniqtuuq

Haviokvik

Hiiktinik
  Hiqtiniq
  Hiiqtiniq
  (Cape Alexander, where the
  creek flows into the ocean)

Hikingogiak

Hingik

Hipliagyuk
  Hipliaryuk

Hitamaiyakvik
  Hitamaiyarviq

Hiukkittaak
  Hiukitak
  Hiuqqittaaq
  (Hiukitak River)

Hivugakhik

Iglukyualik
  Igloryoalik
  Igluryualik

Ihhavik

Ihuktok
  Ehoktok

Ihungak
  Ehongak
  Ihunngaq
  (creek on west side of Arctic
  Sound, north of the mouth
  of the river)

Ikallialuk

Ikallivik
  Iqallivik
  (Footprint River near
  Bay Chimo or camp on the
  east side of Anderson Bay)

Ikaluakpalik
> Iqaluaqpalik
> (place of the big fish monster; usually lives in Napaktolik Lake or McAlpine Lake)

Ikalughiugvik
> Iqalughiurvik
> Iqalukhiurvik

Ikaluit
> Iqaluit
> (Frobisher Bay)

Ikaluktuuk
> Iqaluktuuq

Ikaluktuuttiak
> Ekaluktutiak
> Ikaluktutiak
> Ikalukutuuttiaq
> Iqaluktuuttiaq
> (Cambridge Bay)

Ikalulialuk
> Iqalulialuk
> Ekalulialok
> (large island directly west of Bay Chimo)

Ikalulik
> Iqalulik

Ikigahak
> Ikirahak

Iklukpalik
> Iqalukpilik
> Iqlukpalik
> Iqluqpaliq

Iklukyoalik
> Iklukyualik
> Ikluqyualik
> Iqlukyoalik
> Igluryualik

Iklulik
> Igloolik
> Iglulik

Ikotik

Ikpikyuak
> Ikpikyoak
> Ikpikyuaq

Ilioguyak

Iluilguyak
> Iluilguyaq

Imnaguak
> Imnaruaq

Imnagyuak
> Imnakyoak
> Imnaryuaq

Innaghakvik
> (Perry Island)

Inutkuaghaak
> Inutquaghaaq

Ipikvikhak
> Ipikvighamik
> (Anchor Island)

Itibliagyuk
> Itibliaryuk
> Itipliaryuk
> (lake by Archie Komak's cabin on mainland)

Itighokyoak
> Itigokyuak

Kagiglialok

Kagitaknak
> Kagitagnak
> Qaritarnak
> (Stockport Islands)

Kagitangnak
> Qaritangnak

Kaigayuktuk
> Qairayuktuq

Kainniuktugvik
> Qainniuqturvik

Kalgialok
> Kagiglialok

Kalgilik
> Qalgilik

Kalgilikmi
> Qalriliqmi

Kamaniguak
> Qamaniryuaq

Kangakyuk

Kangighinik
> Kangirhiniq
> (Rankin Inlet)

Kangighuagyuk
> Kangirhuaryuk
> Kangighuaryuk
> (Daniel Moore Bay)

Kangigyuk
> Kangiryuk
> Kangakyuk

Kangikhoakyok
> Kanikhuakyuk
> Kangiqhuaryuk
> (Prince Albert Sound)

Kangikhukyoak
> Kangiqhukyuaq
> (Portage Bay)

Kangiklialuk
> Kangillialuk

Kangikyuaktiak

Kangilgiayok

Kanikhuakyuk
> Kangiqhuaryuk

Kannguyak
> Kangoyak
> Kannguyaq

Kannuyak
> Kanoyak
> Kannuyaq
> (Lewes Island or the island
> due south of Ikalulialuk Island)

Kanuyaokyak

Kapihiliktuuk
> Kapihiliktuk
> Kapihiliktuuq
> (Hope Bay area)

Katimanik
> Katimannak
> (Arctic Sound)

Kaumaugaktuk
> Qaumaugaqtuq
> (Rocking Horse Lake)

Keeliakyuk
> Kiilliaryuk

Kigalghuak

Kiglik

Kiilinnguyak
> Kiilin'nguyaq
> (Kent Penninsula)

Kiillik
> Kiiliq

Kiillinik
> Kiilliniq
> (Victoria Island)

Kikiakaffaaluk

Kikiktagyuak
> Kikiktakyuak
> Qikiqtaryuaq

Kikiktakafaaluk
> Kikiktagaffaluk
> Qikiqakaffaaluk
> (Rideout Island or
> Admiralty Island)

Kikiktakyuak
> Qikiqtaryuaq

Kikitangualik

Kikiuktanayuk
> Qikiqtanayuq

Kikiviakyuk
> Kuukkiviaryuk

Kiiliakyuk

Kilikangualik

Kiluhiktuk
> Kiluhiktuuq
> Kiluhiktuq
> (southern region
> of Bathurst Inlet)

Kimukton
> Kimaktun
> Kemukton
> Kemakton
> Kimaktuun
> (Upper Hiukkittaak River,
> where it gets wide before the
> source lakes)

Kingaagyuk
> Kingakyuk
> Kinngaaryuk

Kingalghuak
> Kingalhuak
> Qingalrhuaq

Kingauk
> Qingauk
> (the community of Bathurst Inlet)

Kingautagyuak
> Qingautaryuaq

Kingmigot

Kitagingnak
> Kitaaginaak

Kitigak
> Kitigaq
> (Kitigak Lake, near
> Ikaluktuuttiak)

Kitunnik
> Qitunnik

Kiunnik
> Qiunnik

Kivyaaktuk
> Kivyaaktuq

Kopilgoktok
> Kupilguktuuk
> Qupilruqtuuq
> (Cape Flinders)

Kugluktuagyuk
> Qurluqtualuk
> (Tree River)

Kugluktualuk

Kugluktuk
> Qurluqtuq
> (Coppermine)

Kugyutik
> Qugyutik

Kuihikvik
> Quihikvik

Kukiviakyok
> Kuukkiviaryuk

Kulgayuk
> Kulgayuk
> (Foggy Bay)

Kunayuk
> Kuunayuk
> (Ellice River)

Kungugyuak
> Kungurjuaq
> Kuururjuaq
> (peninsula that separates
> Elu Inlet from Melville Sound)

Kunnguyak
    Kun'nguyak

Kuugyuak
    Kuukyuak
    Kuukyuaq
    (Perry River)

Kuukkiviagyuk
    Kuukkiviaryuq

Kuugvik
    Kuuvik

Manikyak

Maliktook
    Maulirvik

Mautagina
    Mautarina

Mautak
    Mautaq

Mayauttak
    (Mount George on
     Kent Peninsula)

Mayuattuit
    (Twin Jugs, between Mara
     River and Contwoyto Lake)

Mayugvik
    Mayurvik

Mittimatalik
    (Pond Inlet)

Naarnak
    Naarnaq

Nagyuktuuk
    Nagyuktuuq
    (Charlie Bolt's camp or north of
     Richardson Islands, Coronation
     Gulf)

Nahaoyak

Napaktulik
    Napaaktulik
    Napaktolik
    Napaaqtulik
    (Takiyuk Lake, between
     Contwoyto Lake and Kugluktuk)

Naughigvik
    Naughirvik
    Naokhiurvik
    Nauqhirvik
    (the small channel en route to Daniel
     Moore Bay from Arctic Sound
     or Bay Chimo)

Nauyaat
    (Parry Bay or Repulse Bay)

Nayokhigvik

Niakingovik

Niakkinnguvik
    Niakingovik
    Niaqqinnguvik

Niakuknakyuak
    Niaqurnaqyuaq
    (a hilly area west of Augustus Hills on
     Victoria Island and other places)

Nilaovik

Nuahiakavik Point

Nulahukyuk

Nuvukhit

Ogarvik

Ohingojjat

Oihingak

Oivaktok

Okaliktok
    Ukaliktuk
    Ukaliktok
    Ukaliqtuuq
    (island due west of
     Melborne Island)

Omanak

> Umanak
> Uummannaq
> (point between Grays Bay:
> Agiak and Tree River
> and other places)

Omingmagiuk

> Umingmakyuuk
> (north of Holman Island)

Omingmalik

> Umingmalik
> (Gateshead Island,
> east of Victoria Island)

Ongnak

Ovayualuk

> Uvayualuk

Paakvik

> Paakviq

Paalik

> Padliq
> Palik
> Paalliq
> (Surrey River on Victoria Island
> or Rae River near Kugluktuk)

Paalikyuak

> Paalikyuak
> Padliryoak
> Paalliryuaq
> (Byron Bay on Victoria Island)

Pangnigtung

Pangniqtuuq

> Pangnirtung
> (lake 70 miles northwest
> of Cambridge Bay or a town
> on Baffin Island)

Paonngaktok

> Paon'ngaktok
> Paun'ngaqtuuq

Piginganik

Piginganing

> Piringaning
> Piringaniq

Pitokik

> Pitokik
> Pitaqiq
> Pituqqiq
> (small river 20 miles south of
> Bay Chimo, east side of Bathurst
> Inlet, Kamoayok's cabin)

Sanikiluak

> Sanikiluaq
> (Belcher Islands)

Tagiunnuak

> Taryunuak
> Tariunnuaq
> (Gouldburn Lake behind Brown
> Sound, or near Daniel Moore Bay,
> or Swan Lake at Bathurst Inlet,
> and many other places)

Tahialilungnahik

> Tahialilungnahiq

Tahialuk

> Tahialuk
> (round lake 40 miles
> southeast of Ellice River)

Tahikaffaluk

> Tahigaffalik
> Tahikaffaaluk
> Tahikaffaluq

Tahikyoak

> Tahikyuak
> Tahikyuaq
> Tahiryuaq
> (Contwoyto Lake,
> Ferguson Lake,
> and many others)

Tahipkapfalok

> (lake at source of the
> Hiukkittaak River)

Taliyaguuk
    Taliyaruuk
    Taliyaruuq

Taliuyak
    Taliuyaq

Taloyoak
    Taluryuaq
    (Spence Bay)

Tikigaagyuk
    Tikiraaryuk
    Tikiraaryuq
    Tikiroaryuk

Tikigaagyunnuak
    Tikiraaryunnuaq

Tikigak
    Tikiraq
    (Beechey Point at west
     entrance to Parry Bay)

Tikikgakyok

Tikikvik

Tovyakvik
    Tuvyarvik

Tunullik

Tuulak

Ughuktuuk
    Urhuqtuuq
    (Gjoa Haven)

Ulukhaktuuk
    Ulukhaqtuuq
    (Holman Island)

Umanak
    Umanaq
    Uummannaq
    (point between Grays Bay and
     Tree River and many other areas)

Umiiviit

Umingmaktuuk
    Omingmaktok
    Omingmaktuk
    Umingmaktuuq
    (Bay Chimo, or Washburn Lake
     on Victoria Island)

Umingmakyuuk

Ungahitak
    Unahitak
    Ungahitaq
    (Findlayson Island, between
     Kent Peninsula and Victoria Island)

Ungiivik
    Ungiivik

Uvayuk
    Uvayuq
    (Mount Pelly)

Appendix B
Tuktu and Nogak Project Interview Guide

Questions used as a guide only during semi-directed interviews along with 1:250,000-scale maps.

INTERVIEWEE BIOGRAPHY

1. Where were you born?

2. What year were you born?

3. Who are your parents, spouse, and children?

BACKGROUND

4. What are the Inuinnaqtun names for different kinds of caribou (for example, cows, bulls, and calves, of different ages)?

5. How can you tell the age of a caribou?

6. What do caribou do during different seasons?

7. What do caribou do during the day and at night?

8. How do caribou communicate? When do they make sounds to one another?

COMMUNITY USE

9. Why are caribou important to the Inuit?

10. Do people use caribou today in the same ways that they did long ago?

11. How did people use parts of caribou as medicine long ago?

12. Have you heard if people have different uses for caribou across Nunavut?

LOCAL CARIBOU

13. Where do you see more Barrenland caribou (large and brown)?

14. How many kinds of Barrenland caribou do you see (Queen Maud and Bathurst herds)?

15. Do you see more Barrenland or Island caribou?

16. How can you tell the difference between these caribou?

17. Are there any other kinds of caribou that you see?

18. I've heard that some Barrenland caribou spend the winter near Bathurst Inlet and others go south. Have you seen or heard about this before?

HUNTING

19. Where did you hunt caribou as a young child?

20. Where did you hunt caribou as a young adult?

21. Where do you hunt caribou as an adult?

22. Where is the very best place for hunting? Why? What time of year?

23. What kind of caribou is the best for hunting?

24. Can you tell me about different ways to hunt caribou?

25. Are there certain things that an Inuk is not allowed to do when hunting caribou? (For example, kill more than she or he can eat.)

26. What will happen if a hunter does not follow these rules?

27. What are some Inuit ways to make sure
you come home with lots of caribou?

28. How many caribou do you hunt in a year?

29. How many caribou does your community hunt in a year?

30. Do you remember years when there was
a shortage of caribou? What did you do?

31. Can you tell me about how you skin a caribou?

32. When do you know that you have enough caribou?

33. What do people do when you have unused
caribou or parts of caribou? What did they do long ago?

MIGRATION 34. What time of year and how do cows and bulls
start looking for one another to have calves (rutting)?

35. How many days do the cows and bulls spend
together during the time they are making calves?

36. What time of year do the cows and bulls come together again?

37. When do you first see cows in the spring? What about bulls?

38. Can you use the maps to show us where you
see them and which direction they are moving?

39. Has this changed since long ago?

40. Where do you see caribou in the summer?

41. How are the antlers of a cow and bull different?

42. What time of year do caribou lose their antlers (bulls and cows)?

43. Have you seen areas on the land where there are lots of antlers?

CALVING GROUNDS 44. Where have you seen calving grounds?

45. Why do cows go to this area?

46. Do cows return to where they were born to have their calves?

47. Do cows calve all together in one place or in small groups in different places?

48. When does the first cow arrive at the calving grounds?

49. When does the last cow arrive at the calving grounds?

50. What happens when a calf is born before the cow
reaches the calving grounds?

51. When people are hunting, how can they tell when
a cow is pregnant?

52. How do people feel shooting a pregnant cow?

53. Are unborn calves important to the Inuit for eating?

54. How can people tell when an unborn calf is close to being born?

55. Have you ever seen a calf being born? Can you tell me about it?

56. How old is a cow when she has her first calf?

57. How often does a cow have a calf—every year or every few years?

58. How long do calves stay with the cows?

59. What do cows teach their calves?

MANAGEMENT
ISSUES

60. What are your concerns about calving grounds and mining in this region?

61. What rules should there be about mining and caribou or calving grounds?

62. Are there areas that caribou use where you do not mind mining?

63. What can be done to protect calving grounds?

64. How many kilometres away are caribou when they first sense a small mining camp (fifty people) on the land? What about a large mining camp (two hundred people)?

65. What time of year are caribou most bothered by noise or disturbance?

66. How do caribou act when they are bothered?

67. What do you think should be done so that there are enough caribou for future generations?

PREDATORS

68. Which animals kill caribou?

69. Which animal kills the most caribou?

70. Have you ever seen an animal killing a caribou? What was it like?

71. How do caribou protect themselves and their young from danger?

HEALTH

72. Where have you seen dead or sick caribou?

73. How can you tell when a caribou is sick when you see it from a distance?

74. How can you tell when a caribou is sick when you are skinning it or taking out the insides?

75. Were there more sick caribou today or long ago?

76. How many sick caribou do you see in a year?

77. What are the Inuinnaqtun names to describe sick caribou?

78. Have you seen caribou with green meat? Why is it green?

79. Does caribou meat taste the same all year?

80. How does caribou meat taste from a cow, bull, and calf? Which do you like best?

FEEDING

81. When you are hunting, how do you use the land to find caribou?

82. How do caribou make changes to the land when they are migrating or calving?

83. What do caribou eat?

84. Where do caribou spend the most time eating? (For example, valleys, hillsides.)

85. In this region, where is the best food for caribou found?

CLIMATE 86. How is the weather today compared to long ago?

87. Can you tell me about years when the weather was really cold?

88. What about years when the weather was really warm?

89. Can you tell me about times when the ice broke up early in the spring or formed late in the fall?

90. How does a change in weather influence caribou? Have you noticed differences in the land, water, or snow because of changes in weather?

91. Do caribou like a certain type of snow for travelling?

92. How do caribou know when the snow is going to melt?

CLOSING 93. What is the most interesting thing you have learned about caribou?

94. Do you know of any old stories about caribou?

95. Is there anything else that you would like to share with us?

96. Is there anything we can do to make this interview better?

GERRY ATATAHAK,
SANDRA EYEGETOK,
AND MAY ALGONA,
KUGLUKTUK, 1999.

Glossary

Inuinnaqtun
English

aakturniq
skinning caribou

aghat
grizzly bears

Ahiarmiut
mainland caribou
(from the berries)

amaqqut
wolves

amiiyaiyuq
taking fur off caribou

amiralik
caribou with antlers
that have velvet on them

anguhalluq
young caribou bull

anguniaqpauhiniq
hunter's survival skills

atiqtat
spring caribou
migration northwards

auyalingniq
summer newborn
caribou calves

auyaq
early summer (July–August)

auyiviit
summer caribou grounds

avaalaqiaq
birch and alders

avin'ngat
lemmings

haggaruq/hagganguqtuq
summer caribou (when the
new hair has grown a bit)

haulluut
tool used to get bone marrow
from caribou leg bone, made
of caribou rib

hikhiit
ground squirrels

hila
the weather, the outdoors

iblau
caribou foetus

ilupaaq
inner parka made
from caribou skin

kaiptauyat
mushrooms

kakivak
fish spear

kamngit
caribou skin boots

kan'ngalaq
spring caribou
(when the old hair
has fallen off)

kayuqtuq
red fox

kiahirutilik
cross fox

Kiilliniq (Kiillinik)
    Victoria Island

kikhuk
    fireplace made of rocks

kilumuuqtut
    fall caribou migration
    southwards

kulavak
    caribou cow

maligaghat
    important cultural rules

mipku
    dry meat

mukpauyaq
    fry bread (bannock)

nalluit
    caribou river crossings

niqi
    meat

niqiliqiniq
    butchering meat

niviuvak
    fly

nuiyaaqpak
    barbs between
    caribou antlers

nukatukkaaq
    caribou yearling

nukik
    caribou tendon

nuna
    the land

nurraittuq
    barren caribou cow

nurrat (nogak), nurraq, nurralaaq
    caribou calves

pangniq
    caribou bull

patiq
    marrow from caribou leg bone

piffi
    dry fish

pilaktuq
    slicing caribou meat

pitiktaakkat
    winter caribou

pitquhiit
    beliefs, traditions,
    and customs

pualut
    mitts

qainnijjut
    bone needles

qalviit
    wolverines

qarliit
    pants made
    from caribou skin

quaq
    frozen raw caribou meat

qayuq
    caribou blood soup

qingnit
    meat caches

qiurhungni
    taste of bull caribou
    meat during the rut

qulittaat
    outer parkas made
    from caribou skin

qupilrukhaq
    larvae

talut
 hunting blinds

tiriganniat
 Arctic fox

tuktu
 caribou

tuktuhiuqtut
 caribou hunting

ukiakhaq
 late summer
 (August–September)

ukiakharnitaq/ukiulirmik
 fall caribou

ukiaq
 late fall (October–November)

ukiuq
 winter (December–February)

ulu
 woman's knife

upin'ngaaliq
 spring caribou

upin'ngaaq
 late spring (May–June)

upin'ngakhaq
 early spring (March–April)

uuyuq
 boiled caribou meat

PAUL NICKLEN

PAUL NICKLEN

PAUL NICKLEN

Sources

Interviews

All interviews were conducted during the Tuktu and Nogak Project.

Akana, J., Elder. 1998. Interview by E. Kakolak, D. Keyok, and N. Thorpe, June 8, Umingmaktuuk. Tape recording.

Akana, J., L. Kamoayok, and M. Kaniak, Elders. 1997. Interview by K. Kamoayok and N. Thorpe, July 18, Umingmaktuuk. Tape recording.

Akana, J., L. Kamoayok, M. Kaniak, A. Komak, and E. Panegyuk, Elders. 1998. Interview by J. Akoluk, S. Akoluk, E. Kakolak, K. Kamoayok, V. Klengenberg, P. Niptanatiak, and J. Tikhak Jr., August 9, Hiukkittaak Elder-Youth Camp. Tape recording.

Akana, J., M. Kaniak, and E. Panegyuk Elders. 1998. Interview by N. Haniliak, K. Kamoayok, and N. Thorpe, June 10, Pitokik. Tape recording.

Akana, J., M. Kaniak, A. Komak, and B. Omilgoitok, Elders. 1998. Interview by J. Akoluk, S. Eyegetok, V. Klengenberg, P. Niptanatiak, N. Thorpe, and J. Tikhak Jr., August 10, Hiukkittaak Elder-Youth Camp. Tape recording.

Akoluk, M., Hunter. 1998. Interview by M. Kamingoak and N. Thorpe, May 22, Kingauk. Tape recording.

Algona, B., Hunter. 1999. Interview by S. Eyegetok and N. Thorpe, November 2, Kugluktuk. Tape recording.

Algona, M., Elder. 1999. Interview by S. Eyegetok and N. Thorpe, November 1, Kugluktuk. Tape recording.

Alonak, J., L. Kamoayok, M. Kaniak, and B. Omilgoitok, Elders. 1998. Interview by S. Akoluk, S. Eyegetok, E. Kakolak,

K. Kamoayok, N. Mala, P. Niptanatiak, N. Thorpe, and J. Tikhak Jr., August 8, Hiukkittaak Elder-Youth Camp. Tape recording.

Alonak, J., L. Kamoayok, D. Kaniak, P. Omilgoitok, and E. Panegyuk, Elders. 1998. Interview by S. Akoluk, A. Angivrana, E. Kakolak, K. Kamoayok, and N. Mala, August 10, Hiukkittaak Elder-Youth Camp. Tape recording.

Alonak, J., D. Kaniak, B. Omilgoitok, and P. Omilgoitok, Elders. 1998. Interview by J. Akoluk, A. Angivrana, S. Eyegetok, S. Itkilik, N. Mala, P. Niptanatiak, and N. Thorpe, August 9, Hiukkittaak Elder-Youth Camp. Tape recording.

Analok, F., Elder. 1998. Interview by S. Eyegetok and E. Komak, July 22, Ikaluktuuttiak. Tape recording.

———. 1999. Interview by S. Eyegetok and N. Thorpe, June 12, Ikaluktuuttiak. Tape recording.

Analok, F., J. Analok, M. Angulalik, M. Koihok, L. Kudlak, B. Omilgoitok, and P. Omilgoitok, Elders. 1999. Interview by S. Eyegetok and N. Thorpe, June 15, Ikaluktuuttiak. Tape recording.

Angulalik, B., and A. Komak, Elders. 1998. Interview by S. Eyegetok and E. Komak, July 30, Ikaluktuuttiak. Tape recording.

Angulalik, M., Elder. 1998. Interview by S. Eyegetok and E. Komak, July 24, Ikaluktuuttiak. Tape recording.

Anonymous C, Hunter. 1998. Interview by N. Thorpe, June 3, Kingauk. Tape recording.

Hagialok, J., Elder. 1997. Interview by T. Akoluk, D. Angohaitok, Y. Angohaitok, K. Kamoayok, V. Klengenberg, and N. Thorpe, July 16, Kingauk. Tape recording.

———. 1998. Interview by M. Akoluk, M. Kamingoak, and N. Thorpe, May 26, Kingauk. Tape recording.

Hakongak, N., Hunter. 1998. Interview by M. Omilgoitok and N. Thorpe, May 11, Ikaluktuuttiak. Tape recording.

Haniliak, N., Hunter. 1998. Comments contributed during interview with J. Akana, M. Kaniak, and E. Panegyuk, Elders. Interview by N. Haniliak, K. Kamoayok, and N. Thorpe, June 10, Pitokik. Tape recording.

Hikok, N., Elder. 1999. Interview by S. Eyegetok and N. Thorpe, October 30, Kugluktuk. Tape recording.

Kailik, B., and C. Nalvana, Elders. 1999. Interview by S. Eyegetok and N. Thorpe, November 1, Kugluktuk. Tape recording.

Kamoayok, L., A. Kingnektak, and G. Kuptana, Elders. 1997. Interview by E. Kakolak, K. Kamoayok, D. Kingnektak, G. Panegyuk, N. Thorpe, and J. Tikhak Jr., July 10, Hanigakhik. Tape recording.

Kaosoni, A, and M. Kaosoni, Elders. 1998. Interview by S. Eyegetok and E. Komak, July 22, Ikaluktuuttiak. Tape recording.

Kapolak, A., Hunter. 1998. Interview by K. Ongahak and N. Thorpe, June 5, Kingauk. Tape recording.

Kapolak Haniliak, G., Hunter. 1998. Interview by K. Ongahak and N. Thorpe, June 5, Kingauk. Tape recording.

Kavanna, G., Elder. 1998. Interview by S. Eyegetok, J. Komak, E. Komak, and N. Mala, July 21, Umingmaktuuk. Tape recording.

Keyok, C., Elder. 1998. Interview by E. Kakolak and N. Thorpe, July 29, Umingmaktuuk. Tape recording.

Kingnektak, D., Hunter. 1998. Interview by N. Haniliak, K. Kamoayok, and N. Thorpe, June 13, Umingmaktuuk. Tape recording.

Koihok, M., Elder. 1998. Interview by J. Panioyak and N. Thorpe, May 13, Ikaluktuuttiak. Tape recording.

———. 1999. Interview by S. Eyegetok and N. Thorpe, October 27, Ikaluktuuttiak. Tape recording.

Kuptana, G., Elder. 1998. Interview by E. Kakolak and N. Thorpe, June 7, Umingmaktuuk. Tape recording.

Kuptana, N., Hunter. 1998. Interview by E. Kakolak and N. Thorpe, June 6, Umingmaktuuk. Tape recording.

Maniyogina, J., Elder. 1998. Interview by T. Apsimik, S. Eyegetok, J. Komak, and N. Mala, July 10, Ikaluktuuttiak. Tape recording.

Omilgoitok, B., and P. Omilgoitok, Elders. 1998. Interview by M. Omilgoitok and N. Thorpe, May 14, Ikaluktuuttiak. Tape recording.

———. 1999. Interview by S. Eyegetok and N. Thorpe, October 27, Ikaluktuuttiak. Tape recording.

Panegyuk, G., Hunter. 1997. Comments contributed during interview with L. Kamoayok, A. Kingnektak, and G. Kuptana, Elders. Interview by E. Kakolak, K. Kamoayok, D. Kingnektak, G. Panegyuk, N. Thorpe, and J. Tikhak Jr., July 10, Brown Sound. Tape recording.

TNP Publications

Riedlinger, D., S. Fox, and N. Thorpe. 2001. *Inuit and Inuvialuit knowledge of climate change in the Northwest Territories and Nunavut.* Native Voices in Research: Northern and Native Studies. Edited by J. Oakes and R. Riewe,. Winnipeg: Native Studies Press, University of Manitoba.

Thorpe, N., 1997. The Tuktu and Nogak Project: Inuit knowledge about caribou and calving areas in the Bathurst Inlet region. *InfoNorth* (Arctic) 50, no. 4: 381–84.

———. 1998. The Hiukitak school of tuktu: Collecting Inuit ecological knowledge of caribou and calving areas through an elder youth camp. *InfoNorth* (Arctic) 51, no. 4: 403–8.

———. 2001. Climate and caribou: Inuit knowledge of the impacts of climate change. In *Arctic flora, fauna: Status and conservation,* ed. CAFF (Conservation of Arctic Flora and Fauna), 101. Helsinki: Edita.

———. 2001 (in press). Factors affecting change in Inuit Qaujimajatuqangit and traditional caribou hunting practices in the Kitikmeot region of Nunavut. In *Cultivating Northern landscapes: Knowing and managing animals in the circumpolar North,* ed. D. Anderson and M. Nuttall. Oxford: Berghahn Books.

Thorpe, N., and S. Eyegetok. 2000a. Lessons on the land: The Tuktu and Nogak Project elder-youth camp. Nunavut Tunngavik Incorporated Press. *Ittuaqtuut* 2, no. 2: 32–43.

———. 2000b. The Tuktu and Nogak Project brings elders and youth together. *Native Journal* 9, no. 7: 9.

TNP Workshop Presentations

Thorpe, N. 1997. Inuit knowledge of caribou and calving areas in the Bathurst Inlet region. *5th National Students' Conference on Northern Studies.* Association of Canadian Universities for Northern Studies. Simon Fraser University, Vancouver. November 1997.

———. 2000. Finding balance in times of transition: Inuit recommendations on sustainability in the mineral-rich caribou calving grounds of Nunavut. *12th Inuit Studies Conference.* Aberdeen, Scotland. August 2000.

———. 2000. Starting points for research: Contributions of Inuit knowledge to understanding climate change. *12th Inuit Studies Conference.* Aberdeen, Scotland. August 2000.

———. 2000. Moving forward: Contributions of Inuit knowledge to understanding the impacts of climate on caribou. *51st Arctic Science Conference.* Whitehorse. September 2000.

Thorpe, N., and S. Eyegetok. 2000. Inuit ecological knowledge of climatic influences on caribou. *Workshop on Climate Change Impacts and Adaptation Strategies for Canada's Northern Territories.* Yellowknife. February 2000.

Thorpe, N., S. Eyegetok, and Elder L. Kamoayok. 1999. Inuit ecological knowledge of climatic influences on caribou and calving areas in the Kitikmeot region of Nunavut, Canada. *10th Annual Arctic Ungulate Conference.* University of Tromso, Norway. August 1999.

Thorpe, N., S. Eyegetok, and Elder P. Omilgoitok. 1998. The Tuktu and Nogak Project: Participatory action research in the Kitikmeot region of Nunavut. *Arctic Institute of North America.* University of Calgary. August 1998.

Thorpe, N., D. Riedlinger, S. Fox, and GeoNorth Consultants. 2000. A preliminary assessment of the state of documented traditional and local knowledge research of climate change. *Northern Climate Exchange Workshop.* Whitehorse. September 2000.

TNP Lectures

Thorpe, N. 1997. The importance of youth in the Tuktu and Nogak Project. Umingmaktuuk Elementary School, Umingmaktuuk, July 1997.

———. 1998. Lessons learned: Reflections on conducting cross-cultural and community-based research in the Arctic. Presentation to REM 601, School of Resource and Environmental Management, Simon Fraser University, Burnaby, October 1998.

———. 2001. Research in Inuit knowledge of climate change impacts on caribou in the Kitikmeot region of Nunavut. University of Victoria, Victoria, March 2001.

Thorpe, N., and S. Eyegetok. 1998. Participatory action research in the Arctic: An Inuit and non-Inuit perspective. Simon Fraser University Co-Management Research Group, Vancouver, March 1998.

Thorpe, N., S. Eyegetok, and N. Hakongak. 2000. Thoughtful reflections on Inuit Qaujimajatuqangit (IQ) research. Government of Nunavut, Ikaluktuuttiak, November 2000.

Thorpe, N., N. Hakongak, and Elder M. Koihok. 1998. Youth are the future: Elders and youth for the Tuktu and Nogak Project. Kiiliinik High School, Ikaluktuuttiak, June 1998.

Further Reading

Anderson, D. G. 2000. *Rangifer* and human interests. *10th Arctic Ungulate Conference.* 9–13 August 1999, Tromso, Norway. 20, nos. 2–3: 153–174.

Berkes, F. 1999. *Sacred ecology: Traditional ecological knowledge and resource management.* Philadelphia: Taylor and Francis.

Briggs, J. L. 1970. *Never in anger: Portrait of an Eskimo family.* Cambridge: Harvard University Press.

Cruikshank, J. 1981. Legend and landscape: Convergence of oral and scientific traditions in the Yukon Territory. *Arctic Anthropology* 18, no. 2: 67–93.

deCoccola, R., and P. King. 1989. *The incredible Eskimo: Life among the Barrenland Eskimo.* Surrey, B.C. Hancock House Publishers.

Dene Cultural Institute. 1994. Guidelines for the conduct of participatory community research. In *Traditional ecological knowledge and modern environmental assessment,* ed. B. Sadler and P. Boothroyd, 69–75. Vancouver: Canadian Environmental Assessment Agency, International Association for Impact Assessments, and University of British Columbia, Centre for Human Settlements.

Fehr, A., and W. Hurst. 1996. A seminar on two ways of knowing: Indigenous and scientific knowledge. Inuit Circumpolar Conference and Fisheries Joint Management Committee, 15–17, November, 1996, Inuvik, NWT.

Feit, H., 1988. Self-management and state-management: Forms of knowing and managing Northern wildlife. In *Traditional knowledge and renewable resource management,* ed. M. M. R. Freeman and L. N. Carbyn, 72–85. Edmonton: Canadian Circumpolar Institute.

Ferguson, M. A. D. 1997. Arctic tundra caribou and climatic change: Questions of temporal and spatial scales. *Geoscience Canada* 23, no. 4: 245–52.

Ferguson, M. A. D., R. G. Williamson, and F. Messier. 1998. Inuit knowledge of long term changes in a population of Arctic tundra caribou. *Arctic* 51, no. 3: 201–19.

Fox, S. 1998. Inuit knowledge of climate and climate change. Master's thesis. University of Waterloo.

Fox S. L. 2000. Arctic climate changes. In *Observations of Inuit in the Eastern Canadian Arctic. Arctic Climatology Project, Environmental Working Group Arctic meteorology and climate atlas,* ed. F. Fetterer and V. Radionov. Boulder, CO: National Snow and Ice Data Center. CD-ROM.

Freeman, M. A. 1994. Angry spirits in the landscape. In *Biological implications of global change,* ed. R. Riewe and J. Oakes, 3–4. Canadian Circumpolar Institute, Royal Society of Canada, Association of Canadian Universities for Northern Studies.

Freeman, M .M. R. 1999. The nature and utility of traditional ecological knowledge.http:/www.carc.org/pubs/v20no1.

Gombay, N. 1995. Bowheads and bureaucrats: Indigenous ecological knowledge and natural resource management in Nunavut. Master's thesis, University of Waterloo.

Gordon, B. C. 1996. *People of sunlight, people of starlight: Barrenland archaeology in the Northwest Territories of Canada.* Edited by Archaeological Survey of Canada. Mercury Series. Hull: Canadian Museum of Civilization.

Gunn, A., G. Arlooktoo, and D. Kaomayok. 1988. The contribution of the ecological knowledge of Inuit to wildlife management in the Northwest Territories. In *Traditional knowledge and renewable resource management*, ed. M. M. R. Freeman and L. N. Carbyn, 22–30. Edmonton: Canadian Circumpolar Institute, IUCN Commission on Ecology.

Harper, K. 2000. Inuit writing systems in Nunavut. In *Nunavut: Inuit gain control of their lands and their lives*, ed. J. Dahl, J. Hicks, and P. Jull, 170–79. Copenhagen: International Work Group for Indigenous Affairs.

Huntington, H. P. 1998. Observations on the utility of the semi-directive interview for documenting traditional ecological knowledge. *Arctic* 51, no. 3: 237–42.

Inglis, J. T., ed. 1993. *Traditional ecological knowledge: Concepts and cases*. Ottawa: Canadian Museum of Nature.

International Institute for Sustainable Development and Sachs Harbour. 2000. *Sila Alangotok: Inuit observations on climate change*. 14 min. Videocassette.

Inuit Circumpolar Conference. 1996. Recommendations on the integration of two ways of knowing: Traditional indigenous knowledge and scientific knowledge. In *Seminar on the Documentation and Application of Indigenous Knowledge*, Inuvik.

Ipellie, A. 1997. Thirsty for life: A nomad learns to write and draw. In *Echoing silence: Essays on Arctic narrative*, ed. J. Moss, 93–101. Ottawa: University of Ottawa Press.

Johnson, M., ed. 1992. *LORE: Capturing traditional environmental knowledge*. Ottawa: Dene Cultural Institute, the International Development Research Centre.

Kofinas, G. P. 1998. The costs of power sharing: Community involvement in Canadian porcupine caribou co-man-

agement. Ph.D diss., University of British Columbia.

Krech, S. 1999. *The ecological Indian*. New York: W. W. Norton.

Krupnik, I., and H. Vakhtin. 1997. Indigenous knowledge in modern culture: Siberian Yupik ecological legacy in transition. *Arctic Anthropology* 34, no. 1: 236–52.

Kuhn, R. G., and F. Duerden. 1996. A review of traditional environmental knowledge: An interdisciplinary Canadian perspective. *Culture* 16, no. 1: 71–84.

McDonald, M., L. Arragutainaq, and Z. Novalinga. 1997. *Voices from the Bay: Traditional ecological knowledge of Inuit and Cree in the Hudson Bay bioregion*. Ottawa: Canadian Arctic Resources Committee.

McGhee, R. 1996. *Ancient people of the Arctic*. Vancouver: UBC Press.

Nadasdy, P. 1999. The politics of TEK: Power and the "integration" of knowledge. *Arctic Anthropology* 36, nos. 1–2: 1–18.

Nakashima, D. J. 1986. Inuit knowledge of the ecology of the common eider in Northern Quebec. In *Eider Ducks in Canada*, ed. A. Reed, 102–13. Ottawa: Canadian Wildlife Service.

———. 1993. *Astute observers on the sea ice edge: Inuit knowledge as a basis for Arctic co-management*. Edited by J. T. Inglis, 99–110. Ottawa: International Program on Traditional Ecological Knowledge and International Development Research Centre.

Nelson, R. 1969. *Hunters of the Northern ice*. Chicago: University of Chicago Press.

———. 1980. *Shadow of the hunter: Stories of Eskimo life*. Chicago: University of Chicago Press.

Pinkerton, E. 1994. The future of traditional ecological knowledge and resource management in native communities: Where do we go from here? In *Traditional ecological knowledge and modern environmental assessment*, ed. B. Sadler and P. Boothroyd, 51–60. Vancouver: Canadian Environmental Assessment Agency, International Association for Impact Assessments, and University of British Columbia, Centre for Human Settlements.

Riedlinger, D. 1999. Climate change and the Inuvialuit of Banks Island, NWT: Using traditional environmental knowledge to complement Western science. *InfoNorth* (Arctic) 52, no 4: 430–32.

———. 2000. Inuvialuit knowledge of climate change. In *Pushing the margins: Northern and native research*, ed. J. Oakes, R. Riewe, M. Bennett, and B.Chisholm, 346–55. Winnipeg: Native Studies Press, University of Manitoba.

———. 2001. Community-based assessments of change: Contributions of Inuvialuit knowledge to understanding climate change in the Canadian Arctic. Master's thesis, University of Manitoba.

———. 2001. Responding to climate change in Northern communities: Impacts and adaptations. *InfoNorth* (Arctic) 54, no.1: 96–98.

Riedlinger, D., and F. Berkes. 2001. (in press). Contributions of traditional knowledge to understanding climate change in the Canadian Arctic. *Polar Record*.

Ross, R. 1992. *Dancing with a ghost: Exploring Indian reality*. Toronto: Reed Books.

Spink, J. 1969. Historic Eskimo awareness of past changes in sea level. *Musk-Ox* 5: 37–40.

Stevenson, M. G. 1996. Indigenous knowledge in environmental assessment. *Arctic* 49, no. 3: 278–91.

Stiegelbauer, S. M. 1996. What is an elder? What do elders do?: First Nation elders as teachers in culture-based urban organizations. *Canadian Journal of Native Studies* 16, no. 1: 37–66.

Wenzel, G. W. 1991. *Animal rights, human rights: Ecology, economy and ideology in the Canadian Arctic.* London: Belhaven Press.

———. 1999. Traditional ecological knowledge and Inuit: Reflections on TEK research and ethics. *Arctic* 52, no. 2: 113–24.

NAIKAK HAKONGAK,
NATASHA THORPE, AND
MARGO KADLUN-JONES,
VANCOUVER, 2000.

Illustration Credits

Index

Page numbers for photographs are in **bold type**.

ABOUT THE AUTHORS

KITIKMEOT ELDERS are the many elders and hunters from Kingauk, Umingmaktuuk, Hanigakhik, Ikaluktuuttiak, and Kugluktuk whose voices you hear and faces you see throughout *Thunder on the Tundra*. They have contributed their stories today for generations tomorrow.

SOME OF THE ELDERS, YOUTH, AND RESEARCHERS OF THE TUKTU AND NOGAK PROJECT, IKALUKTUUTTIAK, 1998.

NATASHA THORPE has been fortunate to share tea, time, and tales with Inuit throughout the Kitikmeot. Natasha now lives in Victoria, where she continues to be committed to Inuit Qaujimajatuqangit projects.

SANDRA EYEGETOK has always had a special interest in Inuit culture and Inuit Qaujimajatuqangit projects. Still active with elders in her community, Sandra lives in Ikaluktuuttiak.

NAIKAK HAKONGAK is an avid hunter who spends as much time as possible out on the land while not working as a wildlife officer. Born in Ikaluktuuttiak and raised in Umingmaktuuk, Naikak currently resides in Ikaluktuuttiak.